WRITERS AND THEIR WORK

ISOBEL ARMSTRONG
General Editor

BRYAN LOUGHREY
Advisory Editor

Kingsley Amis

KINGSLEY AMIS

Kingsley Amis

Richard Bradford

Northcote House
in association with the
British Council

For Jenny

© Copyright 1998 by Richard Bradford

First published in 1998 by Northcote House Publishers Ltd, Plymbridge House, Estover Road, Plymouth PL6 7PY, United Kingdom.
Tel: +44 (01752) 202368 Fax: +44 (01752) 202330.

British Library Cataloguing-in-Publication Data
A catalogue record for this book is available from the British Library

ISBN 0-7463-0858-2

Typeset by PDQ Typesetting, Newcastle-under-Lyme
Printed and bound in the United Kingdom

Contents

Biographical Outline   vi

1   Introducing Kingsley Amis   1

2   Method and Development: *Lucky Jim* to
     The Biographer's Moustache   10
     Lucky Jim and the fifties   10
     Unusual realism: the strange fictions of the
     sixties and seventies   19
     The realist returns: *Jake's Thing* to *The Biographer's*
     Moustache   37
     Short stories   50

3   Sex   57

4   Opinions: Politics, Nation, God, Class and Race   72

5   Poetry   92

Notes   110

Select Bibliography   112

Index   116

Biographical Outline

1922   Born 16 April in south London. Brought up in Norbury and educated at local schools.

1934–41   Scholarship to City of London School. Exhibitioner at St John's College, Oxford to read English Literature. Begins a forty-five-year friendship with Philip Larkin, to whom he dedicated his first novel, *Lucky Jim*.

1942–5   Lieutenant in Royal Corps of Signals. Serves in Normandy, Belgium and Germany.

1945   Returns to Oxford. Meets John Wain, whose first novel *Hurry on Down* (Secker & Warburg, 1953) is regarded as one of the archetypal 'angry' texts. The two were apparently 'united in homage to Larkin'. Amis gains a first in English (1947) and continues as research student. BLitt thesis on 'English Non-Dramatic Poetry 1850–1900 and the Victorian Reading Public' was unsuccessful.

1947   *Bright November* (poems) published by the Fortune Press, whose proprietor was R. A. Caton. L. S. Caton, a plagiaristic academic, slips Hitchcock-style through Amis's novels until he is killed off with ironic finality in *The Anti-Death League* (1966).

1948   Marries Hilary Ann Bardwell ('Hilly').

1949   Editor, with James Michie, of *Oxford Poetry*.

1949–61   Lecturer in English, University College, Swansea. His head of department, James Kinsley, described him as 'a loyal colleague and provocative teacher'. His life in South Wales provides the background for *That Uncertain Feeling* (1955), *The Evans Country* (poems, 1962) and *The Old Devils* (1986).

1951   Begins work on *Lucky Jim*. Meets Dylan Thomas – a rather sad experience described in his essay 'An Evening with Dylan Thomas'.

1953   *A Frame of Mind: 18 Poems*.

1954   *Lucky Jim*. Still his most popular novel. The book went through ten impressions in the year of its publication. Prior to publication, extracts were read on BBC Radio programme *First Reading*, of which John Wain was the editor.

1955   *That Uncertain Feeling*. *Lucky Jim* wins Somerset Maugham Award and provides funds for Amis's visit to Portugal (*I Like It Here*).

1956   *A Case of Samples: Poems 1945–1956*. Amis's poems published in *New Lines* edited by Robert Conquest, the original 'Movement' volume.

1957   *Socialism and the Intellectuals*. Reflects Amis's brand of ambivalent socialism.

1958   *I Like It Here*. *Lucky Jim* filmed with Ian Carmichael as Jim, Terry-Thomas as Bertrand and Hugh Griffith as Neddy Welch.

1958–9   Visiting Fellow in Creative Writing, Princeton University. Gives lectures on science fiction and collects materials for *One Fat Englishman*. Amis's encounter with an unendearing Jack Kerouac is recorded in the essay 'Who Needs No Introduction'.

1960   *Take a Girl Like You*. *New Maps of Hell* based on Princeton Lectures. An essay called 'Lone Voices' contains his now famous comment on the expansion of British Higher Education that 'MORE WILL MEAN WORSE', and in it he judges the 'Angry Young Men' and the Movement to be little more than 'digest compiling categories'.

1961–3   Fellow and Director of Studies in English, Peterhouse, Cambridge. Donald Davie described Amis's time there as a 'brief but eventful and unhappy period', and F. R. Leavis was caused to reflect upon the state of an English faculty which could employ a 'pornographer'. Amis himself describes the period in the essay 'No More Parades'.

1961   *Spectrum: A Science Fiction Anthology* edited by Amis and Robert Conquest. Three further volumes followed in

	1962, 1963 and 1965.
1962	*My Enemy's Enemy* (short stories). *That Uncertain Feeling* filmed as *Only Two Can Play* with Peter Sellers as John Lewis.
1963	*One Fat Englishman.* Gives up university teaching, and thereafter lived in and around London.
1965	*The Egyptologists*, with Robert Conquest. Marries Elizabeth Jane Howard.
1966	*The Anti-Death League.*
1967	*A Look Round the Estate: Poems 1957–1967.* 'Why Lucky Jim Turned Right' – an essay explaining his rejection of socialism and the attractions of the Conservative Party. Visiting Professor at Vanderbilt University, Nashville. Collects material for US section of *I Want It Now.*
1968	*I Want It Now. Colonel Sun*, a James Bond novel, under the pseudonym of Robert Markham.
1969	*The Green Man.*
1970	*What Became of Jane Austen: and Other Questions* (essays). *Take a Girl Like You* filmed as a sixties sex comedy, with Hayley Mills as Jenny, Noel Harrison as Patrick, and a screenplay by George Melly.
1971	*Girl 20.*
1973	*The Riverside Villas Murder.*
1974	*Ending Up.*
1975	*Rudyard Kipling and his World*, short critical biography.
1976	*The Alteration* awarded John W. Campbell award for science fiction.
1978	*Jake's Thing.*
1979	*Collected Poems 1944–79.* His (published) paper on *An Arts Policy?* at the Conservative Party Conference reiterates his long-held belief that art, particularly literary art, should be popular, accessible and, thus, self-financing.
1980	*Collected Short Stories* and *Russian Hide-and-Seek.*
1981	Awarded CBE. Separates from Elizabeth Jane Howard.
1982	Moves in with Hilary and her third husband, Alastair Boyd, Lord Kilmarnock.
1984	*Stanley and the Women*, seen by many reviewers as the final confirmation of a lurking, misogynistic tendency.
1986	*The Old Devils* awarded the Booker Prize.

1987   *The Crime of the Century,* first published as a six-part
        murder mystery in the *Sunday Times* 1975.
1988   *Difficulties with Girls.*
1990   *The Folks That Live on the Hill.* Becomes Sir Kingsley
        Amis.
1991   *Memoirs.*
1992   *The Russian Girl.*
1994   *You Can't Do Both.*
1995   *The Biographer's Moustache.* On 22 October Amis dies in
        University College Hospital, London.
1997   *The King's English: A Guide to Modern Usage.*

1

Introducing Kingsley Amis

Kingsley Amis was born in a south London nursing home on 16 April 1922. He was an only child and from infant to early teenage years he lived with his parents at 16 Buckingham Gardens, Norbury SW16. His environment was comfortably suburban, lower middle class and largely unaffected by the intellectual and political reverberations of the 1920s and 1930s. Amis's familial relationships were routinely imperfect and non-traumatic. His parents were almost attached to Baptist non-conformity, but they did not push Kingsley towards any particular brand of Christian morality or belief. Amis himself had no belief in God: 'not the first beginning of one, not a shred, and never have had as far back as I can remember' (in 'Godforsaken', *The Amis Collection*, 1990).

He attended the City of London School as a scholarship boy and, again on a scholarship, went up to St John's College, Oxford, in April 1941. There he met his life-long friend Philip Larkin. Amis, Larkin and a group of similarly inclined young men spent their spare time boozing, playing and telling jokes and moaning about the English curriculum. Amis joined the student branch of the Communist Party: 'at least...it involved girls, not very nice looking ones, though' (*Memoirs*, 37). By 1942 he was editing the Labour Club *Bulletin*.

After four terms in Oxford Amis was drafted into the Royal Corps of Signals where he served as first lieutenant until October 1945. He landed in Normandy two weeks after D-Day and took part in the allied push through France and Belgium, mostly behind the front line.

Amis returned to Oxford in 1945 and gained a first in English in 1947. He enrolled for a BLitt research degree and in 1950 submitted a thesis on 'English Non-Dramatic Poetry 1850–1900 and the Victorian Reading Public', which was failed. By 1950 he had also published a brief volume of poems, *Bright November* (1947), met and married Hilary Ann Bardwell (Hilly), had two children and secured a lectureship in English at University College, Swansea. Their third child, Sally, was born in 1954.

These are the skeletal facts of Amis's life up to the publication of the novel that made him famous. *Lucky Jim* (1954) was influenced directly and tangentially by all of these events. Indeed everything that happened to him up to and including the writing of the novel created the prototype Amis, as man and writer; the basis for all subsequent deviations, extensions and reversals.

We can begin with beliefs and affiliations. Amis enjoyed literature, but not all of it. His evaluative instincts were based upon a combination of temperament, a respect for accessibility and a deep loathing for self-indulgent experiment. In his failed thesis (which he abbreviated and published as an article in *Essays on Criticism* in 1952) he divided Victorian poets into two groups: those who considered the interests and predispositions of their potential audience (particularly Rossetti, Tennyson and Browning) and those who were more concerned with their own technical accomplishments and ideas (particularly Hopkins, Meredith and Morris). Amis's argument was, for its time, iconoclastic. He did not question the stylistic abilities or the imaginative range of either group, but he focused upon a poet's ability to open his skill to a reader who wishes to be challenged but not patronized.

This principle remained at the centre of his own tastes as a reader and his work as a writer and critic. Thirty years later he wrote of Tennyson that his poetry

> turned out to be resistant to modern techniques of literary criticism. It holds no interesting ambiguities, intentional or unintentional; there are no puzzles, no 'levels of meaning' within it, it just is. All the critic can say about most of it comes down to, 'Look at this. Good (or bad), isn't it?' (*Tennyson*, 1973)

This is the Amis manifesto. He admires transparency not as a simplistic tendency to ignore form, but as a technique of blending form and content so skilfully that the intelligent reader will not require the professional critic to tell him how, and how well, the one supports the other.

Amis's opinions would appear to be largely consistent with those of the 'Movement'. This was a group of poets, including Amis, Larkin, Robert Conquest, D. J. Enright and Donald Davie, who during the 1950s attempted to break free from what they regarded as the stranglehold that modernism held upon 'serious' English poetry. The Movement poets, and Amis particularly, are frequently categorized and misunderstood as regressives, as writers who adapt pre-modernist techniques to contemporary conditions. Amis is best understood as an accessible radical. As I shall show in chapter 5 his poetry frequently catches the reader between open registers of transparency and familiarity and unnerving shadows of obliqueness and chaos.

His fiction is even more difficult to categorize. Amis's first novel was never published. *The Legacy*, completed in 1948, tells the story of a 19 year old called Kingsley Amis who has to decide between two lives: one with Jane whom he loves and who admires his ambitions as a poet; and one with Stephanie of whom his family approves and who will guarantee his father's £30,000 legacy and his place in the family firm. The novel was a mixture of Edwardian social commentary and contemporary existential crisis, without a trace of humour. Amis was later to reflect that his failure to find a publisher was propitious. It meant that he had to try something completely different, and *Lucky Jim* was born.

Lucky Jim is the eighteenth-century picaresque novel reborn in the 1950s. Amis chose the setting of a provincial university mainly because he worked in one, but he claims that the idea actually predated his job in Swansea. In 1946 he visited Larkin at Leicester University, where the latter worked as a librarian. In the Senior Common Room he witnessed something that was real but unreal; groups of academics 'sitting, standing, talking, laughing, reading, drifting in and out, drinking coffee'. All of these were normal, routine activities but it seemed to Amis as if they were happening in a world quite removed from its non-academic counterpart. 'Not that it was awful – well, only a bit, it was strange and sort of *developed*, a whole mode of existence no one had got on to from outside, like the SS in 1940, say?' (*Memoirs*, 56).

3

The university is not so much the novel's satirical target; rather it provides a fruitful counterpoint for the activities, ambitions and mindset of Jim Dixon. Jim is intelligent but he is not really interested in big ideas. He detests the intellectual pretensions of many of his colleagues, yet he promotes no alternative code of behaviour or system of belief. His own interests seem to focus upon drink, jazz, getting the right girl and a well-paid job somewhere else. He succeeds in his ambitions, and to a degree the novel was an overnight success because it satisfied the desire of many readers to escape from, and ridicule, the moribund conventions and pretensions of middle England.

Lucky Jim is frequently cited as a key text in the 1950s phenomenon of the Angry Young Men. The heroes of John Osborne's *Look Back in Anger* (1956), John Braine's *Room at the Top* (1957) and John Wain's *Hurry on Down* (1953) are variously clever, resourceful, frustrated and angry. Their state of mind is diagnostic; it tells us something about the tensions created within the new England after the post-war Labour government, about class mobility, promiscuity and radical ideas. But Jim's anger symbolizes nothing in particular, and it never lasts for very long. He is not really malicious, he never takes anything very seriously, and his state of mind is certainly not a channel for contemporary angst or intellectual unease. He does not care about these things.

What makes *Lucky Jim* important both as a literary event in its own right and as a prototype for much of Amis's later work is the relationship between Jim and his narrator, which I will discuss in detail in the next chapter. They are like a narrative double-act. Jim performs the jokes. By accident and design he finds himself at the centre of mildly farcical yet plausibly realistic situations, surrounded by an abundance of satirical targets: pomposity, pretension, cultural élitism, unwarranted self-regard. But Jim alone never really operates as an agent of satire. It is the dynamic relationship between Jim and a presence who comments sardonically on the state of things and who records Jim's thoughts that provides the novel with its energy and its satirical edge.

The novel is significant not simply because it indicates a post-war shift towards anti-modernism, nor because it mirrors the social and intellectual state of 1950s England, but because it revived a trend that had been largely absent from mainstream literature since the eighteenth century, and which can best be described as serious comedy.

Comedy is the literary genre that most effectively resists abstract definition. Our responses to literary evocations of death, despair or isolation are, in a civilized and decent way, predictable. Comedy is far more personal and divisive. When tragedy reduces us to tears or when we empathize with the moral or existential crisis of a character, we are participating in the fiction; we know that our feelings are part of the game of pretence. But if we share a writer's sense of humour, if we laugh, our feeling of satisfaction transcends its fictional source. And our sense of outrage and offence when something that we value is mocked is equally genuine.

Amis, in *Lucky Jim*, had discovered his *métier*. Practically all of his subsequent work involves a substratum of comedy. His more experimental, apocalyptic fictions such as *The Anti-Death League* (1966) and *The Alteration* (1976) are unlikely to leave the reader shaking with hilarity, but to regard this kind of relief as the only function of comedy is to relegate it to the lower division of literary endeavour that it has largely occupied since the Romantic period. Amis's brand of comedy brings together elements of the familiar, the routine and the dangerously absurd. It returns us to a realm of the comic which seems to have been lost to 'serious' literature since Swift's *A Modest Proposal* and Pope's *The Dunciad*.

Since *Lucky Jim* Amis has been one of Britain's most popular novelists, but he has not always drawn the praise of serious critics. W. Somerset Maugham regarded *Lucky Jim* as symptomatic of a kind of anarchic, immoral opportunism. Gilbert Phelps in 'The Novel Today' regards Amis as a cheap populist: *I Like It Here* (1958), 'frequently falls back on lavatory jokes'; '*Take a Girl Like You* (1960)... is slapdash in style and confused and negative in tone'; *The Green Man* (1969) 'contains many of Amis's most irritating characteristics, among them the scoffing, sometimes hectoring tone, the schoolboyish dirty jokes, the joyless sex'.[1] When Amis moved from Swansea to a fellowship at Peterhouse, Cambridge, in 1961, F. R. Leavis was dismayed that his university had sunk low enough to employ a 'pornographer'.

Roger Fowler in *Linguistics and the Novel* regards Amis's creation of Jenny Bunn (*Take a Girl Like You*) as symptomatic of his class-bound, misogynistic tendencies: he had created an 'ignorant provincial virgin come South'.[2] Legions of reviewers found *Jake's Thing* (1978) and *Stanley and the Women* (1984) to be indefensibly sexist diatribes, which, alongside their hatred of women, reserved generous levels of contempt for the young, social workers and anything and anyone non-English. *Jake's Thing* made Tom Paulin feel unwell: 'Reading Amis's prose is like getting kicked in the stomach – I found myself retching at its sheer awfulness'.[3]

These critics might seem to have different reasons for disliking Amis's fiction, but I would suggest that their collective unease is prompted as much by his manner as by his treatment of particular topics. In many respected, canonized novels, major characters frequently embody ideas and behavioural characteristics that some people will find disagreeable. But we generally recognize that we are responding to a created figure in a fictional world, that the character is not a channel for the author's particular prejudices or attitudes. With Amis, such tolerance is made difficult by our awareness of a presence who hovers behind or around the main character, always ready to pounce and never willing to allow a piece of dialogue or a solemn proclamation to get past without first puncturing whatever pretension to absolute validity it might carry with it. Many of Amis's principal characters have disagreeable qualities: inveterate lechery, confident verbal sadism, a selfish disregard for other people's feelings. Frequently, however, they will share with the figure who creates the text a state of sardonic scepticism, combined with an almost habitual tendency to ridicule or dismiss other people's ideas without proposing alternatives. In short, Amis tends to suggest a collusive sympathy between the principal character and the person who created him (they are predominantly male), with the result that his novels can seem to some readers to be exercises in dismissive prejudice.

My thesis, which I shall adumbrate here and substantiate in the following chapters, is that Amis's novels, as well as involving humour and satire, raise the question of what the function of literature is.

Amis, like many of his peers and associates, was anti-modernist. Gabriel Josipovici distinguishes between modernist and realist fiction as follows: 'The act of perception or the act of consciousness is never a neutral one ... Proust and Homer and Virginia Woolf are all aware of this, but the traditional novel appears to ignore it. As a result it implicitly assumes that the world and the world as we are made conscious of it are one'.[4] Josipovici's distinction is based upon the premise that reality is not a fixed continuum of things and ideas waiting to be apprehended but that the process of apprehension, particularly in its reliance upon language, is a significant feature of reality. Amis would probably agree with him on this point, but he would certainly challenge his contention that literature must continually foreground and self-consciously explore its own techniques in order to capture the delicate relationship between perception and consciousness.

Amis's fiction is realist or traditionalist in the sense that you do not need to know a great deal about literature or literary theory to understand or enjoy it. But at the same time it accomplishes exactly the effect that Josipivici argues is beyond the range of traditional writing. It shows us the world through language, while showing us that a substantial part of this world is made from language.

His novels fall into two categories. The first group, beginning with *Lucky Jim*, are overtly realist. They are contemporary. They involve locutionary habits, states of mind and frames of reference that are transparent and familiar. But these novels are not mimetic. They are halls of mirrors, in which the reader is invited to recognize aspects of their own situation, yet which gradually, subtly, distort this experience. In *The Old Devils* (1986), for example, the third-person narrator remains apparently indifferent but switches the narrative focus from character to character in each chapter. This is a routine strategy of traditional fiction, but Amis complicates it by killing the most charismatic and influential of these figures in the middle of the novel. The effect of this upon the other characters is, in the realist manner, largely predictable. But Alun Weaver's departure also has an effect upon the relationship between these characters and their narrator, and consequently upon the relationship between the novel and the reader. The characters' world has changed and, in a manner that defies the easy prescriptions of modernism, so has the reader's experience of their world. The narrator is still there – an easy, sardonic, jovial presence – but it is as if the characters' fictional response to death communicates itself to him, and then to us.

Amis's other brand of fiction mixes genres. Time frames are altered, the plausible is combined with the weirdly implausible. In *The Green Man* (1969), the narrator meets God in his sitting room. The effect of this is all the more peculiar because the narrator has successfully convinced us that he is an agnostic, coherent, sane, and very real presence. We feel that his world is ours, and suddenly it cannot be ours.

David Lodge has argued that traditional fiction offers the critic more problems than its modernist counterpart because it 'works by concealing the art by which it is produced, and invites discussion in terms of content rather than form, ethics and thematics rather than poetics and aesthetics'.[5] Many of Amis's critics have accepted the invitation. In the following chapters I shall show that Amis's fiction can only be properly understood through an appreciation of its form. The relationship between Jim Dixon and his narrator, the effect upon the narrative fabric of the 'death' of Alun Weaver, the appearance of God in Maurice Allington's sitting room: all of these involve a degree of artistic concealment, but, when we uncover the method behind the effect, it offers us an exhibition of the nature of fabrication that is just as intriguing as the device-baring strategies of the modernists.

His two modes of writing share a number of characteristics. First of all they are unaligned. They never promote a particular belief or ideology. An error shared by many of Amis's reviewers and critics, particularly the hostile ones, is to align what is known of Amis the man with the more shadowy controller of the text. Amis the man has always been a candid, provocative presence. Since the fifties he has contributed book reviews, and articles on practically everything else, to many of the British tabloids, broadsheets and literary magazines. His collected essays in *What Became of Jane Austen?* (1971) and *The Amis Collection* are full of autobiographical recollections and accounts, supplemented by his own *Memoirs* (1991). His shift from moderate left-wing affiliations towards conservatism in the

1960s became a public event. Amis's energetic desire to continually tell us what he thinks is partly authentic and partly an elaborate subterfuge. The title of his 1967 essay 'Why Lucky Jim Turned Right' is a red herring. The essay is about Amis, but by this time he was familiar with the critical tendency to regard his fictional characters as undisguised versions of himself. He was always ready to play along with the myth, but the essay itself disposes of it. Amis turned right not because the Tories had the answers to our problems but because socialism in his view claimed to have all the answers: that all moral, ethical and straightforward political dilemmas could be resolved by rote. Amis hated systems, forms of belief and analysis – intellectual, moral, sociological – which claim to tell us how life works, and this characteristic of Amis the man holds the key to a proper understanding of his fiction.

His talent for making his characters and situations unnervingly real was not employed just as an exercise in mimesis. He wanted to invite the reader into the text, to make us react, sympathetically or angrily, to what his characters did and said. What he would not do was to turn the novel itself into either a defence or a condemnation of a particular system of ideas. There is evil and cruelty in some of his novels, but he does not patronize the reader by reminding us of what these things are, nor by offering the novel as an all-inclusive explanation of why they exist and how we might deal with them.

Amis does not write parables or submit disguised solutions to personal, intellectual or political problems. The only form of ideology that he does offer his readers is his own style of writing: it is serious *because* it is funny. Comedy for Amis was not simply a form of light relief: it was a necessary condition of writing fiction. In *Stanley and the Women*, his most depressing and unfunny book, Amis contemplates insanity as an enclosed, impenetrable state, where distinctions between the real and the unreal no longer exist. Making up stories and employing every ounce of one's literary talent to make them seem real was one guarantee of sanity; and through Nash, the psychoanalyst, he offers another, which is perhaps his own most essential literary and indeed philosophical precept.

> The rewards for being sane may not be very many but knowing what's funny is one of them. And that's an end of the matter.

2

Method and Development
Lucky Jim (1954) to The Biographer's Moustache (1995)

LUCKY JIM AND THE FIFTIES

Lucky Jim piloted Amis from relative obscurity to nationwide fame. It went through ten impressions in 1954 and has never gone out of print. It became a benchmark of 1950s iconoclasm and its targets were numerous.

Jim Dixon is, like Amis, a young untenured don in a provincial university, though his subject is history rather than English. He becomes the agent for a fast-moving, almost random sequence of satirical attacks. His boss, Professor Neddy Welch, is a semi-articulate buffoon with a taste for madrigal music and a commitment to the organic simplicities of medieval England. He is the archetype of head-in-the-sand academia, and his satirical function is embedded in the contrast between his own absurdist persona and the presentation of his context as something that the contemporary reader recognizes as very real. Bertrand, Neddy's son, is an artist of loud pretensions, fashionable leftish sympathies and limitless social ambitions. Like Neddy, he is absurd but not quite implausible. Jim's colleague and occasional girlfriend, Margaret Peel, is theatrically neurotic, sometimes simulating the kind of nervous breakdown favoured by intellectuals, but only when this is tactically propitious. She is a personification of the mid-fifties taste for psychoanalytic depth, European existentialism and very English calculation.

Lucky Jim became a bestseller partly because it pre-empted *Private Eye* in its rebellious swipe at middle-class posturing and self-regard, but its principal source of popularity was its hero, Jim Dixon. Evelyn Waugh's early heroes – Pennyfeather and

Boot particularly – find themselves bounced from one set of absurd circumstances to another and respond with an almost complicit degree of tragi-comic stoicism. Unlike them or Wodehouse's Wooster or even Orwell's George Bowling, Jim refuses to play the hapless victim. Jim is a successful opportunist. His 'luck' enables him to escape the mundane hypocrisies of provincial academia for a well-paid job in industry, and he takes with him Christine, Bertrand's stunningly attractive and unpretentious girlfriend. He is neither malicious, cunning nor corrupt, but at the same time he does not promote any particular system of morality or belief. Contemporary readers liked him not because of what he represented but because of what he did. He exposed the hypocrisies and absurdities of middle-class life while securing for himself a satisfactory position within it.

How did Amis successfully reconcile such apparently contradictory perspectives and characteristics? He did so through the cunning relationship between Jim and his third-person narrator. One *Times Literary Supplement* commentator (17 February 1956) stated that the novel had spread the impression of redbrick universities as peopled by 'beerdrinking scholarship louts', lecherous social climbers who 'wouldn't know a napkin from a chimney piece'. W. Somerset Maugham in the *Sunday Times* 'Books of the Year' feature for Christmas 1954 was even more distressed, claiming that *Lucky Jim* was symptomatic of impending social and cultural anarchy. Graduates such as Jim would insinuate themselves into the educational, political and cultural infrastructure: 'they are scum...I look upon myself as fortunate that I shall not live to see it'. What troubles these critics is Jim's ability to ridicule practically everything and promote nothing, apart from a kind of selfish philistinism. This impression is made all the more effective by the formal structure of the novel.

David Lodge[1] has noted a comic tension between what he calls Jim's 'inner and outer worlds'; the outer consisting mainly of deferential relations with a circle of characters, including the Welches and Margaret, whose opinions will affect his present and future life; the inner, of Jim's actual feelings and thoughts, including the desire to ram a necklace bead up Margaret's nose and plant his head of department in a lavatory basin. At the end

11

the two worlds merge. He tells them what he thinks and makes his triumphant exit. Jim functions like a first-person narrator, in that the reader is offered only his perspective upon the world and the story. But the third-person mode excuses Jim from having to justify, celebrate or even explain his thoughts and acts to the reader. More significantly the alliance between Jim and his narrator grants him a level of sophistication and control that belies his status as the disempowered victim of a farce. It is as though there are two Jims: one inside the narrative, struggling with his own impatience, frustration and feelings of contempt; the other controlling and orchestrating the narrative, ensuring that the reader will share his perspective – on the idiocies of Welches and the pretensions of Bertrand and Margaret. Jim the character is 'lucky'; he gets the girl, the job and he gets out. But the other Jim has all the time been exacting a kind of revenge on the characters and the world that seemed intent on denying him these prizes.

Chapter 20 begins as follows:

> What, finally, is the practical application of all of this? Can anything be done to halt, or even to hinder, the process I have described? I say to you that something can be done by each of us here tonight. Each of us can resolve to do something, every day, to resist the application of manufactured standards, to protest against ugly articles of furniture and table-ware, to speak out against sham architecture, to resist the importation into more and more public places of loudspeakers relaying the Light Programme...

We already know that Jim has been coerced by Professor Welch into giving a public lecture on the decline of contemporary culture. This could well be it. He finishes this particular discourse by reminding the audience of how much better life had been in the 'village-type communities' of medieval England, and then the narrator takes over.

> With a long, jabbering belch, Dixon got up from the chair where he'd been writing this and did his ape imitation all round the room. With one arm bent at the elbow so that the fingers brushed the armpit .... he wove with bent knees and hunched, rocking shoulders across to the bed, upon which he jumped up and down a few times, gibbering to himself.

The joke is clear enough. The 'Merrie England' thesis of the lecture is, for 1950s Britain, about as useful and valid as the case for a return to the instinctive, prelinguistic community of our simian ancestors. Jim is both the joker and the audience – there is no-one else in the room – but for the reader his gesture is given greater satirical edge by the narrator's method of first making us suspect that Jim is actually delivering the lecture. They are working together. Jim's joke with himself is a vital component of the narrator's joke with the reader.

In chapter 1 we find Jim in the passenger seat of Welch's car, being driven to the latter's home 'for tea'. The narrator has just disclosed Jim's thoughts on the significance of his forthcoming article on medieval shipbuilding, its 'niggling mindlessness, its funereal parade of yawn-enforcing facts, the pseudo-light it threw upon non-problems'. Jim then proceeds to offer a hypocritical recommendation of its scholarly qualities to his boss, and again the narrator takes over.

> Unable to finish his sentence, [Jim] looked to his left again to find a man's face staring into his own from about nine inches away. The face, which filled with alarm as he gazed, belonged to the driver of a van which Welch had elected to pass on a sharp bend between two stone walls. A huge bus now swung into view from further round the bend. Welch slowed slightly, thus ensuring that they would still be next to the van when the bus reached them, and said with decision: 'Well, that ought to do nicely, I should say.'

The narrator's prose is beautifully timed and balanced. He describes the progress of the vehicles and the expressions of their occupants with sardonic indifference and meticulous detail. The effect is comparable to a film played in slow motion, and Welch's concluding statement injects a darkly comic tone: we can never be sure if he is commenting on the success of his near-suicidal driving or whether he regards this kind of motor-ballet as routine and is referring back to the satisfactory status of Jim's article.

The narrator does not simply show us the comic interplay between Jim's inner and outer worlds; he functions rather as Jim's superhuman alter ego. He times and structures the narrative with the same deft, sardonic irony that Jim would have used if he had told his own story. Amis always admired and enjoyed the novels of Henry Fielding, and it is possible to find the imprint of Fielding in the style of *Lucky Jim*. In 1749, when Fielding published *Tom Jones*, the English novel lacked an established stylistic tradition. The third-person narrative existed, but novelists had not yet developed a reliable menu of devices which would hide its intrinsically paradoxical features. On the one hand the world presented by the narrator was plausibly familiar: characters dressed, behaved and spoke like real people. On the other, the person who disclosed this believable scenario was unbelievable: how could someone who knows so much about this world not be part of it? Fielding did not resolve this paradox; rather it became part of his stylistic fabric. In Book 10, chapter 5 of *Tom Jones*, for example, the narrator ushers his characters out into the garden to allow himself enough non-fictional time to digress on the state of things with the reader. The question of how the narrator could be both there and not there, of how he could be at once constrained by apparently real events yet able to assume a superhuman control over them was left open.

Amis adapted Fielding's dynamic, seat-of-the-pants tension between fictional and non-fictional levels to the structure of *Lucky Jim*, and the parallels become particularly evident in the episode of the university dance occupying chapters 10–12. The events of the episode – Jim chats with Margaret, they meet Bertrand and Christine, Jim dances with Christine – involve no more that about twenty minutes of 'real time', but the dialogue and locative descriptions of these events are threaded into lengthy third-person commentaries via the thoughts and feelings of Jim.

The following is a brief example of this technique, from chapter 10:

> Christine's aim, he imagined, had been to show off the emphasis of her natural colouring and skin-texture. The result was painfully successful, making everybody else look an assemblage of granulated half-tones. For a moment, as she and Bertrand came up, Dixon caught her eye, and although it held nothing for him he wanted to cast himself down behind the protective wall of skirts and trousers, or, better, pull the collar of his dinner-jacket over his head and run out into the street. He'd read somewhere, or been told, that someone like Aristotle or I. A. Richards had said that the sight of beauty makes us want to move towards it. Aristotle or I. A. Richards had been wrong about that, hadn't he?

14

The pace and timing of the prose is pure Jim Dixon; his nervous desire for Christine blends routinely into his farcical, self-mocking mood. Even the projection of his thoughts into the profound disquisitions of Richards or Aristotle is tempered by ridicule: he can't remember and doesn't really care about which of them said it.

The dance episode can be classed as realistic, in the sense that the stylistic devices are transparent rather than self-referential; but at the same time it is chaotically unrealistic. The passage quoted above is fitted in between Margaret's phatic announcement of the arrival of Bertrand and Christine – 'Ah, here they are' – and Bertrand's pretentious greeting – 'Well, what goes forward people?' – a real time period of less than a minute. Jim's prelinguistic musings in this period might have involved brief flickers of admiration and panic, but the narrator offers us a cool, laconic reflection, rendered in a style that we know Jim Dixon would have used, had he been watching a film of the events, able to freeze the frame and offer a commentary.

At the end of the novel, Christine and Jim are boarding the train for London and they encounter the Welch family on the platform.

> He saw that not only were Welch and Bertrand both present, but Welch's fishing-hat and Bertrand's beret were there too. The beret, however, was on Welch's head, the fishing-hat on Bertrand's. In these guises, and standing rigid with popping eyes, as both were, they had a look of being Gide and Lytton Strachey, represented in waxwork form by a prentice hand.

The narrator tells us that Jim 'drew in breath to denounce them both', but instead he collapses with laughter. ' "You're...' he said. "He's..." '. We will never know if Jim intended to offer the Welches a description of their unintended parody of Gide and Strachey, whether the confluence of low farce and high cultural allusions occurs to Jim or just to the narrator. Our uncertainty is a key element of the novel's success. It.was felt by Somerset Maugham, who found himself unable to properly distinguish between the foolish but lucky hero and another presence who has an impressive command of language, culture and scholarship but, like Jim, takes none of them too seriously. For Maugham they had become the same, philistine voice – 'scum' as he put it – but for many readers, who turned the book into an overnight bestseller, Jim and his narrator showed that it was possible to write a very clever novel which has no respect for being clever.

In *Lucky Jim* Amis allows the emphasis to shift incessantly between the narrator's skilful orchestration of events and the narrator as, partly, Jim Dixon, the hapless participant. Each of Amis's next four novels draws upon an element of this stylistic mixture, but, probably because they substitute a part for the whole, none was as successful.

That Uncertain Feeling (1955) is a first-person account by South Wales librarian John Lewis, involving adultery, class and Welsh culture. Lewis is a combination of Jim Dixon – while lacking the former's social, sexual and alcoholic restraints – and Jim's narrator. Like the latter, Lewis will disrupt the reader's perceptual faculties by blurring the boundaries between the narrative and the events narrated. At a play by his social and sexual rival Gareth Probert – a thinly disguised parody of Dylan Thomas – the dramatic dialogue is elided with the actual exchange between Lewis and his potential mistress.

> 'I was talking a mouthful of grass under the still hornbeam.'
> 'Amen is it? RIP, right?'
> 'Aren't you getting a bit fed up with this?'
> The last speaker was Elizabeth.

Amis's switch, in this novel, to first-person narrative is tactical rather than innovative. We learn more about Lewis than we did about Jim, particularly his guilt, desires, ambitions, and occasional self-loathing. It is a novel which addresses the socio-sexual mores of the 1950s far more seriously than did its predecessor, and its style is its vehicle. The above passage is from the first part of the novel, in which Lewis is driven by a desire for professional advancement and extra-marital sex. It becomes evident that his stylistic flair – cynical, satirical, dismissive – is a symptom of his condition. His habit of showing off to the reader, of playfully orchestrating the narrative, mirrors his tendency to deceive his wife, his friends and his colleagues. The novel opens with the following pronouncement. ' "The Bevan ticket", I said, "has expired, and will have to be renewed" '. A middle-aged woman in a 'mitre-like hat' responds. 'Mrs Bevan said she just wanted one like the one she had out last time'. The dialogue continues for a while, its context unspecified and its verbal layers offering mildly surreal suggestions of politics and sex. (Are Nye Bevan's left-wing ideas no longer relevant? Is Mrs Bevan thinking about extra-marital activity?) Lewis eventually discloses the ticket as the one issued by the dreary library in which he works. This sense of Lewis loading his account of his, as he sees it, drab existence with ironic counter-patterns of more engaging and intriguing matters sets the tone for the rest of the novel. It provides a stylistic parallel to his actual attempts to transform his condition with adultery and social climbing. In the closing chapter, Lewis returns to his family and discards his social and professional ambitions. Concurrently his account becomes much more candid and transparent, and far less entertaining.

Amis acknowledges *I Like It Here* (1958) to be 'by common consent my worst novel'. Its central character, Garnet Bowen, takes his family to Portugal for a month, his visit sponsored by his publisher who has sent Bowen in search of the enigmatic and reclusive writer Wulfstan Strether. Through Bowen, Amis canvasses his own irritations with foreign travel, teaching, the pretensions of modernist writing, publishers and the literary in-crowd. This kind of satirical edge had been a key element of his first two novels, but in this one it becomes a sequence of well-executed jokes and set pieces. On the ferry, for example, Bowen reflects, for about four pages, on classes he used to give for foreign students on 'Contemporary British Novelists'. The jokes concentrate on his students' enthusiasm for 'Grim Grin' (Graham Greene), 'Ifflen Voff' (Evelyn Waugh) and 'Shem Shoice' (James Joyce), and the narrative is sustained by the one that Bowen can't decode, 'Edge-Crown', who turns out to be A. J. Cronin.

Like Jim Dixon, Bowen maintains a shifty alliance with his third-person narrator, but the effect is dissipated by the impression that neither of them is confident about the direction or purpose of the story. Its general theme is language – literary language, different languages, the ability of language to disrupt meaning – but, by detaching Bowen and the narrator from the web of familiar discourses that permeates his first two novels, Amis seems constantly to be searching for another comic episode that will provide them with a linguistic punch line.

17

Chapter 9 consists entirely of Bowen, and the narrator, alone in the rented cottage. It begins with Bowen attempting to rewrite his unfinished 'play'. He can't do the dialogue because it is just dialogue; he has a constant desire to fill in the gaps with descriptions of what happens. He gives up and reads part of the manuscript by a man who claims to be Wulfstan Strether, which reads like a synthetic pastiche of Henry James, D. H. Lawrence and Dylan Thomas; endless sentences laden with plant and animal symbolism strangle tiny pieces of monosyllabic dialogue. The chapter itself carries a degree of symbolism. Obviously Bowen should be writing a novel, not a play, but he can't because of the novel he is in. He is stuck in a house in a foreign country, estranged from the interplay between everyday life and his own language upon which good novelists feed. Look what happened to Strether who has spent most of his life in Portugal: his novel is in English, but it has become detached from the way that people use English. For Garnet Bowen read Kingsley Amis, who has written a novel about the conditions in which he would find it very difficult to write a novel.

The relationship between Jim Dixon and his narrator is, in *Take a Girl Like You* (1960), given a mildly experimental twist. Patrick Standish is John Lewis transplanted to the English middle class; his third-person narrator, like Jim's, is a version of his own witty, cynical persona. Jenny Bunn, whom Patrick pursues with the shameless energy of Samuel Richardson's Lovelace, is Amis's first three-dimensional woman character: her narrator tells us what she thinks and feels (and we will consider Amis's exploration of style and gender in the next chapter).

Roger Micheldene of *One Fat Englishman* (1963) begins chapter 11 with a silent recitation of Latin poetry, including brief comments on how difficult it is to recognize line-endings in time-based classical metres. We are back with the playful device of reader orientation, recalling Jim's lecture and Lewis's account of Probert's play. In this case it becomes slowly apparent that Micheldene's habit of mentally rehearsing his high-cultural reference points – including Evelyn Waugh's celebration of Pre-Raphaelite theory – has a single, functional purpose: it is his only reliable method of preventing premature ejaculation. Micheldene brings together all the tastes, prejudices and shameful excesses that Amis's previous male characters had

18

managed to control or subdue. His wit and satirical competence migrate, like Jim's, into the third-person narrative, but the effect is far less endearing. The cohabitants of Micheldene's story, Helene his occasional mistress, Macher the beat-movement novelist, and an assembly of stereotypical Americans, are presented as fully deserving of the fat man's limitless contempt. The narrator/character alliance of *Lucky Jim* involved a playfully ambiguous juggling of perspectives. With *One Fat Englishman*, the reader is unsettled by the fact that the narrator seems intent on confirming Micheldene's view of himself and the rest of the world as united in the pursuit of lust, greed, and self-promotion.

Lewis, Bowen, Micheldene, Bunn and Standish, are, potentially, different characters, but their similarity is guaranteed by Amis's habit of pillaging and reshaping the stylistic components of *Lucky Jim*. After *One Fat Englishman*, Amis took his fiction in two directions. One strand maintained the comic-realism of the fifties, but Amis began to expand its boundaries and effects; he began to test his stylistic repertoire against the complexity of its subjects. The other was more innovative and unpredictable: it was realistic in that style never obscured the specifics of narrative sequence or characterization; it was experimental in that Amis employed his stylistic skills to make the patently fantastic disturbingly plausible. I shall deal with the second strand first.

UNUSUAL REALISM: THE STRANGE FICTIONS OF THE SIXTIES AND SEVENTIES

Few writers can have undergone a change so startling and unexpected as that which occurred between the end of *One Fat Englishman* and the beginning of *The Anti-Death League* (1966). The latter has no central character. The narrator is an unpredictable presence, sometimes probing the emotional depths of a character and sometimes supplying only stage-directions during lengthy passages of dialogue. The narrative takes a strange and compelling route through the lives of four men and two women. Its focus is a military establishment and its rural environs; its subject, ostensibly, is the development of a secret weapon known as 'Operation Apollo' and the activities of

19

an anonymous practical joker, the founder of the 'League'. The novel's setting is England around the time of its publication, but Amis's narrator discloses the events and the context in a sinister, selective manner. At one level the novel returns us to the social realism of the fifties writing. The dialogue is peppered with contemporary locutions and references, and the third-person specifications of mid-sixties habits, decor and dress are comfortably accurate. At the same time these minutiae of setting and period are undermined by an equally powerful sense of time having been stopped and setting being informed by a nightmarish conjunction of the familiar and the apocalyptic.

The novel begins in what seem to be the grounds of a country house. Two women, unnamed, are watching an exercise in animal intrigue. A black cat is crouched in a shadow, while a bird, aware of the cat's presence, wheels in the air in an attempt to protect her nest from the hostile carnivore. Another group, 'three men in uniform', arrive and one comments: '"Look at this," he said. "Did you ever see anything like it?"' He is referring not to the cat and the bird but to a water tower built in the same sinister, gothic style as the house. A low-flying aircraft draws the attention of both groups. It also startles the cat whose flight across the grass causes one of the women and one of the men to glance at each other. 'Just when the girl turned and looked at the tall young man it was as if the sun went out for an instant. He flinched and drew in his breath almost with a cry'.

Throughout the passage there is a subtle and uncertain interplay between the reader's perception of the events and what we assume is felt by the participants. For the reader, the passage is crowded with ominous symbols: the cat and bird, the aircraft and the gothic tower all carry resonances of looming and imminent terror. These events register for the participants ambiguously. The young man's brief sensation of shock is immediately absorbed by routine currencies of comment and conversation. Is he taken in by the gloomy presence of the water tower, the shock of the aircraft, or the girl?

'I never took our James for a student of architecture, did you Moti?' asked the senior of the three officers... 'He was really admiring something far more worth a young man's while than cold stones, am I right James?'
'Well yes. I thought she was wonderful, didn't you? Extraordinary

eyes. But sort of blank and frightened.'

Is she frightened? She never explicitly betrays anxiety or fear to her companion, but we are invited to regard the young man and the girl as particularly sensitive to the ominous symbols and the eerie atmosphere. The narrator is playing a game with the reader. The events disclosed to us are portentous, loaded with premonitory signs: or at least they would be if the reader were disposed to interpret them in this way.

The young officer and the girl are eventually disclosed as James Churchill and Catherine Casement, whose love affair is a central feature of the narrative. James is an officer involved with Operation Apollo, and Catherine is recovering from a nervous breakdown. As a means of reintroducing herself to normal life, she takes a part-time job at the village pub, where, eighty pages later, they meet again.

> 'I knew you straight away.'
> She could not stop herself saying, 'And I knew you straight away.'
> 'I know.'

Their encounter seems to both of them inevitable, predetermined, and their relationship begins almost immediately. A few days later we find them strolling through the countryside. James

> looked at her and past her together, so that girl, trees and stream formed a unity. She turned her head and looked at him. He knew for certain that in some way this moment had become inevitable ever since that other moment the afternoon he first saw her when he had looked at a patch of country similar to this one and thought of her. He felt his heart lift. This had never happened to him before, and he was surprised at how physical the sensation was.

The correspondences between the two passages multiply. They sit down in the 'deep shadow' of the trees, not unlike the 'deep shadow' in which the cat was crouched. They undress, and he watches as her expression 'grew wilder', 'less human'. They make love, and the gothic symbolism of their first meeting seems to have been sympathetically decoded by fate. However, during their post-coital embrace James discovers a lump in her breast, which will eventually be diagnosed as cancer.

In Amis's earlier novels, questions of what happens next or of why the relationship succeeds or fails are predicated upon the reader's awareness of the contingencies of non-fictional life. In *The Anti-Death League*, the narrator obliges us to wonder if there are forces at work in the narrative, and by implication in the real world, that are not grounded in circumstance. The narrator achieves a fine balance between the world perceived from the inside by its characters and from the outside by the reader. We are told nothing that the characters would not know, and we share the question of whether these events and conditions carry a significance beyond their status as cold empirical detail. By the end of the novel the question remains open, for all of us. The novel concludes with its characters in a state of temporary remission: the development of Catherine's cancer could have been arrested; James, who had gone into a coma, is revived; Operation Apollo is deferred but not forgotten. But, to remind the reader that nightmares do not always have comforting conclusions, the closing pages offer an unnerving sequence of twists upon a narrative subplot.

Major Ayscue, the regimental padre, is a man of God whose public persona is that of the liberal Christian. Privately he has substituted a conventional perception of God for a faith based upon aesthetics. His favourite composer, one Thomas Roughhead, appears to have created patterns of symmetry and resonance that bespeak, perhaps, evidence of cosmic design. Ayscue's faith rests upon the possibility of the creation of a beautiful order from the plentiful chaos of sound. At the end of the novel, inspired no doubt by the improved condition of James and Catherine, he stages a performance of a Roughhead piece. At the end of the performance he prays, principally for the health of Catherine.

> Whenever he had prayed before it had been like talking into an empty room, into a telephone with nobody at the other end. But this time...somebody was at the end of the telephone, not saying anything, nowhere near that, but listening.

Outside, his dog, his closest companion, has been disturbed by the music. She panics, slips her collar and is run over by a lorry.

The Anti-Death League involves Amis in a provocative engagement with the novel of ideas. Structurally, it recalls Aldous Huxley's imposition of baroque coherence upon contingency in works such as *Point Counter Point* and *Eyeless in Gaza*, and it prompts comparisons with the later novels of Waugh in which the author's Catholic faith insinuates itself into the otherwise unfettered nihilism of the modern world. Amis provokes and unsettles these precedents. He invites the reader to make sense of the fictional world while continually undermining this process. The fabric of daily life is not unlike that of the fifties novels, but it is shot through with potentially sinister elements that neither the narrator nor the characters find it necessary to explain. The pub in which Catherine works is disarmingly familiar.

> The landlord was a redfaced man of fifty called Eames. He wore a short brown beard, grown as a contribution to the modernizing of the premises... 'I'm putting you in the lounge bar to start with, Mrs Casement, because the trade isn't very heavy there, except sometimes at weekends, and there'll be someone else on then as well to give you a hand. You get a very nice person in the lounge...'

This could be the Home Counties of *Take a Girl Like You*, five years on. Beards, in 1966, symbolized pseudo-radical modernity; in ironic contrast with the enduring conventions of the village pub, whose lounge is visited at weekends by 'nice persons' probably down from London. Minutes later Catherine comes face to face with James, described as a 'young man in khaki standing on the other side of the counter'. The phrase 'in khaki' is slipped into the account as if it were no more unusual than Eames's beard, and the fact that soldiers in Britain had not worn uniform for off-duty socializing since the war is not explained. Nor, for that matter, is Operation Apollo. The civilians know about it and the soldiers talk of its imminence and dangers, but no one reflects upon the reasons for it. Its target might well be communist China, yet no references to a cold war crisis, or indeed to global or national politics, the state of Britain, or to anything or anywhere outside the immediate location of the narrative ever informs the dialogue or the third-person account. The effect is not unrealistic. If the situation of a novel is contemporary there is no reason why the narrator or the characters should fold into the text detailed explanations of the socio-political context: contextual inferences, such as the status of Eames's beard, cement the situational complicity between the text and the reader. But, for the reader of *The Anti-Death League*, familiarity has been visited by disturbing elements of the unfamiliar, the apocalyptic. Amis's achievement is to blend these so seamlessly into a network of commonplace occurrences. The contemporary reader feels at home in the world of the novel, but the feeling is attended by an anxiety, a need to know exactly what is going on. And it is by this means that Amis draws us into the anxieties of Churchill and Ayscue; the narrator, by making us experience their world as ours yet not ours, obliges us to share their desire to interpret signs, impose a coherence, we hope benign, upon familiar phenomena that no longer make sense.

Modernist fiction is celebrated for its ability to make us think again about the routine relationship between language and the things, feelings and events that language mediates. The interior monologue, made famous by Joyce and Woolf, shows us that when we translate our thought processes into the organized structures of language we do a grave injustice to their fluid, chaotic actuality. Joyce, in *Ulysses*, shows us Dublin on a single day through a kaleidoscopic lens: practically every established post-sixteenth-century prose style is employed to demonstrate that a single sequence of events can effectively be altered by the manner in which we choose to disclose it. Amis is not a modernist. Joyce and Woolf would, initially, confuse and mystify a reader whose diet of fiction had been limited to the novels of the eighteenth and nineteenth centuries; Amis would not. But at the same time Amis shares with the modernists a capacity to use fiction as a challenge to familiar expectations and perceptions. Unlike the modernists, he does not abandon the established techniques of realist fiction. Rather he shows us that these techniques have not exhausted their capacity to unsettle the reader's preconceived notions of reality. The following is from Amis's discussion of G. K. Chesterton's *The Man Who Was Thursday* but it could stand as an accurate summary of the technical achievements of *The Anti-Death League*.

> – an air of unreality that is not the same thing as implausibility (though there is implausibility here and there as well), a feeling that the world we see and hear and touch is a flimsy veil that only just manages to cover up a deeper and far more awful reality, a sense, in fact, of impending 'apocalypse' in the literal meaning of 'uncovering'.[2]

In *The Green Man* (1969) Amis interweaves the plausible and the implausible in a way that has rarely been achieved before or since in English fiction. Maurice Allington is the first-person narrator and he renews our acquaintance with the selfish, lecherous, drunken, cynical attributes of his fifties predecessors, only worse. He owns a hotel and restaurant, called The Green Man, forty miles from London and within easy reach for the culinary sophisticates of Cambridge. We know the location of The Green Man, the price of its eel soup and the unsound quality of its white Burgundies before we encounter Maurice: an excerpt from *The Good Food Guide* precedes the narrative. Maurice begins:

> The point about white Burgundies is that I hate them myself. I take whatever my wine supplier will let me have at a good price (which I would never dream of doing with any other drinkable). I enjoyed seeing those glasses of Chablis or Pouilly Fuissé, so closely resembling a blend of cold chalk soup and alum cordial with an additive or two to bring it to the colour of children's pee, being peered and sniffed at, rolled round the shrinking tongue and forced down somehow by parties of young technology dons from Cambridge or junior television producers and their girls. Minor, harmless compensations of this sort are all too rare in a modern innkeeper's day.

This mixture of candour and detail sets the standard for Maurice's account. In the next five pages he tells of his family: his wife Joyce, Amy his 13-year-old daughter from his first marriage, his 80-year-old father. He confides in the reader: he drinks a bottle of whisky a day and he intends to have sex with 'tall blonde and full-breasted Diana' the wife of his closest friend. All of this is shot through with asides on the varying qualities of his pork and salmon dishes, the gullish philistinism of his clientele and the 'hypocrisy' of having *sauce vinaigrette* with avocado pears. We might not like Maurice Allington but he is disarmingly real.

Why, we wonder, does Maurice feel the need to confess, albeit unapologetically, while embedding these confidences in meticulous detail? He leaves nothing out of his account partly because he needs to reassure himself that his story is true. Maurice is given to entertaining his guests, particularly Americans, with the tale of Thomas Underhill, who owned the inn in the seventeenth century, made a pact with the devil, sacrificed his wife and monitored the murderous activities of a

25

wood creature from whom the inn takes its name. Maurice's tale to the reader involves his discovering that the legend is true and that Underhill has returned.

For the first half of the narrative Maurice allows us to share his initial scepticism. He has seen figures, shapes, oddly coloured birds. But he is in a peculiar condition. His father has died, his domestic life is a mess and he drinks too much. Soon after he has seduced Diana, she too sees a terrifying, not-quite-human figure in the lane; but so what? This is an exciting element of their shared deception: 'she had demonstrated a fresh superiority by seeing a ghost when I had not. Did she now think she had really seen a ghost?'

In chapter 4 any ambiguities are removed. From his sitting room Maurice witnesses the freezing of time and space. 'Down to the left, forty or fifty yards away across the grass, a couple of waxworks cast their shadows, the seated one with a hand stuck out in the direction of something, probably a cup of tea, that the standing one was offering it, and were Lucy and Nick', his daughter-in-law and son. In his sitting room is a young man, whom Maurice describes with customary attention to detail: about 28, clean-shaven, good teeth, silver-grey suit, black knitted tie, humorous but not very trustworthy face. The young man is God.

> 'Are you a messenger?' I asked.
> 'No. I decided to come uh...in person.'
> 'I see. Can I offer you a drink?'
> 'Yes thank you, I'm fully corporeal. I was going to warn you against making the mistake of supposing that I come from inside your mind, but you've saved me that trouble. I'll join you in a little Scotch, if I may.'

Maurice achieves a remarkable balance between the cool verisimilitude of his account and its totally implausible subject. He passes God a glass of Scotch.

> The hand that came up and took it, and the wrist and lower forearm that disappeared into the silver-grey shirt cuff, were by no means complete, so that the fingers clicked against the glass, and at the same time I caught a whiff of that worst odour in the world, which I had not smelt since accompanying a party of Free French through the Falaise Gap in 1944. In a moment it was gone, and fingers, hand and everything else were as they had been before.

26

'That was unnecessary,' I said, sitting down again.
'Don't believe it old boy. Puts things on the right footing between us.
This isn't just a social call, you know. Cheers.'

The quality of this passage exists in its combination of empirical detail and something that Maurice cannot describe. The hand and arm are 'by no means complete' but the precise nature of this phenomenon is registered only in allusions that Maurice can share with the reader: the fingers click against the glass as if Christ's nails are still there and the 'worst odour' recalls equally indescribable events from the last war.

How is a contemporary reader supposed to respond to Maurice's narrative? Michael Radcliffe in his *Times* review argues that 'In relating supernatural hallucinations to the psychology of a selfish and unhappy man [Amis] has moved towards a tough metaphor of disintegration'.[3] This is an attempt to situate *The Green Man* in a recognizable category of prose fiction, perhaps recalling Waugh's *The Ordeal of Gilbert Pinfold* or more recent work by Iris Murdoch, such as *The Bell* (1958) and *The Time of the Angels* (1966), in which contemporary middle-class culture is contrasted with the religious ideals that it would seem to have repudiated. Radcliffe assumes that Maurice is exploring his mental condition, that seeing God and ghosts in a Cambridgeshire inn can only be a metaphor for the contemporary condition of unsecured morality and existential uncertainty: Maurice has gone mad. Amis disagrees: 'It all really happens...none of what is recounted happens only in the hero's mind'.[4] Maurice's God is not a hallucination nor a symptom of his departing sanity. If we don't believe that Maurice has spoken with God then nor can we believe anything else that he tells us about his daughter, his father's death, his failed marriage and his adulterous inclinations. Maurice folds the plausible and the implausible into the same discourse, and Amis, a writer who has eschewed the techniques of modernism, has created a novel which explores its own identity far more perplexingly than any modernist text ever has.

Several times throughout his narrative Maurice contemplates what is happening in his own life – his father's death, his acts of sexual betrayal, his relationships with those closest to him – and considers what an artist would do with these phenomena: 'A man has only to feel some emotion, any emotion, anything differentiated at all, and spend a minute speculating on how this would be rendered in a novel...to grasp the pitiful inadequacy of all prose fiction to the task it sets itself' (ch. 1). This sounds a trifle insubordinate since, were it not for Amis's competent mastery of the task he had set himself, Maurice and his emotions would not exist. Later, in chapter 2, Maurice again rattles the fictional cage and specifies, at least in his view, the nature of the novelist's task: 'Father, Joyce, Underhill, Margaret, the wood creature, Amy, Diana: a novelist would represent all these as somehow related, somehow all parts of some single puzzle which some one key would somehow unlock'. The novelist is like God; he creates the world of his fictional text and monitors the thoughts and actions of its inhabitants. God himself expands on this thesis. Maurice asks

> 'The whole thing's a game, is it?' I had returned with the drinks.
> 'In the sense that it's not a particularly, uh...edifying or significant business, it is, yes. In other ways it's not unlike an art and a work of art rolled into one...'
> 'Your friend Milton, for instance.' The young man nodded over at my bookshelves. 'He caught onto the idea of the work of art and the game and the rules and so forth.'

The narrator insists on the truth of his account and contrasts it with the inadequacy of fiction, while God compares his own confessedly imperfect enterprises with the creation of a literary text. And the reader, by this point, might begin to question the purpose of these self-referential folds. God's enigmatic allusion to Milton holds a clue.

In *Paradise Lost* Milton explored the boundaries between indisputable truth and literary fabrication. He did not alter the narrative of the book of Genesis but he turned its distant, transcendent presences, including God and Satan, into very human dramatis personae. The contemporary reader was invited to recognize God as a figure with distressingly familiar limitations and motivations, and Satan is presented, in Shakespearean terms, as a failed overreacher who echoes the tragic reality of human motivation. Parallels with Amis's humanized God are clear enough, but they go deeper than that. Adam, Milton's principal human character, leaves the narrative with an address to the Angel Michael, and so the reader, on what they have witnessed.

> Greatly instructed I shall hence depart.
> Greatly in peace of thought, and have my fill
> Of knowledge, what this vessel can contain;
> Beyond which was my folly to aspire.
>
> (Bk ll XII, 557–60)

Adam's statement is subtly and ambiguously interposed with the projected thoughts of the reader. Adam, a participant in the text, departs from it in a compliant, unquestioning condition. The reader, who has been presented with a God who dissembles as readily as King Lear, leaves the text in a less composed state. The most intriguing parallel between *Paradise Lost* and *The Green Man* exists in their shared ability to unsettle rather than suspend disbelief. Milton tests the seventeenth-century reader's faith. He fictionalizes the resolutely non-fictional and challenges the accepted parallels between this world and what lies beyond it. Similarly, Amis's twentieth-century reader – Christian, agnostic, atheist or whatever – is confronted with a text which at once replicates and disrupts prior conceptions of actuality.

In his conversation with God Maurice is allowed one question, and he asks if there is an afterlife.

> 'I suppose there's nothing else you could call it, really. It's nothing like here or anything you've ever imagined and I can't describe it to you. But you'll never be free of me, while this lot lasts.'
> 'Isn't it going to last forever?'
> 'That's a further question, but never mind. The answer is that I don't know. I'll have to see. I mean that.'

On the last page of the novel Maurice reflects on this.

> Death was my only means of getting away for good from this body and all its pseudo-symptoms of disease and fear, from the constant awareness of this body, from this person, from his ruthlessness and sentimentality and ineffective, insincere impracticable notions of behaving better, from attending to my own thoughts and from counting in thousands to smother them from my face in the glass. He said I would never be free of him as long as the world lasted, and I believed him, but when I died I would be free of Maurice Allington for longer than that.

The passage resonates with echoes of Adam's closing speech. Adam folds two levels of meaning into the same words. He will 'depart' from the text, and eventually from life; the reader, for

29

the time being, will depart only from the text. But the reader, unlike Adam, will not have had his 'fill of knowledge' because 'this vessel', this poem, encourages him to 'aspire' 'beyond' it.

Similarly Maurice creates an uneasy tension between what he says about his own condition and our knowledge that he does not, beyond his fictional persona, exist. Is this Maurice contemplating his actual death, or is it Amis playing a game with the parallels between the span of a single human life and the similarly finite duration of a fictional text? Maurice will die and for the reader at the end of the novel he has died. As God has reminded him Maurice will never be free of Him 'while this lot lasts'. Quite so, but is 'this lot' Maurice's existential condition or is it Kingsley Amis's novel, which will last until page 175; at which point we too will be free of Maurice and his God 'for longer than that'. These questions are projected into our reading of Maurice's speech by the very nature of the text that precedes it; which involves a constant tension between the plausible and the implausible, the verifiably tangible and the self-evidently unreal. Maurice's obsessive concern with locative detail and empirical fact is commensurate with his cynical view of artistic pretensions: his story, he reminds us, is true. His touchingly sincere conversations with his daughter, his candid documentation of his desire for drink and sex, his disarmingly honest disclosure of his hypocrisies and prejudices are non-fictional in the sense that Maurice Allington is as three-dimensionally real as anyone we are likely to meet. But Maurice's familiar, naturalistic style is at odds with the text's frequent excursions into the fantastic. Even a reader who believes in God will find it difficult to suspend disbelief in reported conversations with a seventeenth-century Satanist, encounters with a manic wood creature and in the Almighty, Scotch in hand, conceding that he has not yet made up his mind about the nature of eternity.

Amis's achievement in *The Green Man* is to show that conventional fiction can operate in territory that modernism has claimed as its own. Modernist fiction was by no means defunct in the 1960s. In B. S. Johnson's *Alberto Angelo* (1964) the 'author' continually interrupts the narrative to reflect upon the process of constructing it, and in his *The Unfortunates* (1969) the narrative itself consists of twenty-seven loose-leaf sections which can be read in any order. Andrew Sinclair's *Gog* (1967) takes us on a tour of contemporary England and employs a post-Joycean kaleidoscope of narrative forms, including the critical essay, the comic strip and the film script. The common feature of these books is a desire to demystify the processes of writing and reading fiction. The modernists expose the dishonesty of fiction by self-consciously exploring and dismantling its techniques and in doing so they disrupt the reader's inclination to go through the text to the actuality of its story and its characters. Amis turns this process on its head; the fabric of his text is seamless, almost transparent, but none of its readers can claim to have experienced the reality that it so persuasively discloses. *The Anti-Death League* and *The Green Man* establish a precedent for Amis's other experiments with prose fiction, in which he injects elements of the fantastic and the unreal into the credible fabric of the text.

The Alteration (1976) invites comparisons with Huxley's *Brave New World* and Orwell's *Nineteen Eighty-Four*. It is set in England in 1976, but this is 1976 as it would have been if Henry VIII's elder brother Arthur had lived on to become king, married Catherine of Aragon and sired a line of alternative Tudors. England and those parts of Europe uncolonized by the Islamic enemy have remained Catholic, and the religious institution has effectively replaced secular power. It tells the story of Hubert Anvil, 10 years old and the best boy soprano in living memory. The alteration is the surgical castration of Hubert which will preserve his magnificent voice and secure for him respect and position in a world where the arts are the esteemed preserve of the Vatican hierarchy. The vaguely liberal alternative to Catholic Europe is 'New England' an independent settlement on the American continent, populated by Red Indians and descendants of European exiles and dissidents, including W. Shakespeare. The narrative focuses upon Hubert's attempt to avoid the alteration by finding sanctuary in the New England embassy.

Its closest literary relative is not Orwell's or Huxley's novels, but Swift's *A Modest Proposal*. Orwell and Huxley allegorized a society and a human condition that were at the time of writing distressingly possible. Swift did not seriously envisage cannibalism as the capitalist solution for Irish poverty and Amis is not predicting or warning us against the outcome of a Papal takeover bid, but with both we find ourselves disturbed by neat

31

symmetries between what common sense tells us can never happen and what we recognize as horribly endemic features of humanity.

Throughout the novel Amis continually counterposes familiar stylistic and cultural features with bizarre contexts. Pope John XXIV, with whom Hubert and his father are granted an audience, is a Yorkshireman who addresses Hubert as 'lad' and explains the serving of an English tea: 'Our stomach still hasn't accustomed itself to the local muck...Shall we be mother?' The scholar, Abbot Thynne, has ordered 'a new commentary on the *De Existentiae Natura* of Monsignor Jean-Paul Sartre, the French Jesuit'. Hubert sings Mozart's Second Requiem (K878) 'the crown of his middle age' to the congregation in Coverly (which could be Canterbury or Coventry) Cathedral, whose walls carry 'Blake's still brilliant frescoes depicting St Augustine's progress through England', 'Holman Hunt's oil painting of the martyrdom of St George' and the 'excessively traditionalist almost archaizing' Ecce Homo mosaic by David Hockney.

The dialogue is a mixture of informal syntax and locutions drawn from practically every strand of post-seventeenth-century English. Alongside these comic reshufflings of history, we encounter reminders that some things never change. Hubert's escape bid through London sends him into the clutches of Jacob and his assistant Jack. Jacob inhabits the setting and the language of Dickens's Fagin. At one point he quotes Shylock – 'Have we not eyes...' – but Hubert has never heard of the exiled Shakespeare, nor it seems does he appreciate that Jews are forced to live in hiding. Hubert's enlightenment continues when he eventually reaches the New England embassy where the liberal Pastor Williams explains the status of the servant Abraham, an American Indian. 'His mind is less capable to be developed than yours or mine, because his brain is smaller, as our scientists have proved. To mingle with him truly is impossible, and no good can come of trying to. That's why, under God's guidance, we in New England have a design we call separateness' (ch. 5).

The narrative centres upon Hubert, and as a channel between the text and the reader he is disturbingly effective. In a sense his experience of the text mirrors our own. He is intellectually precocious, well educated in the discourses and abstract codes of his adult mentors, but he has no real experience of the life that these discourses pretend to explain or justify. We accompany him in his escape bid and for both of us the fabric of his world is unravelled: the institutionalized veneration of high art is paralleled by an endemic and unchallenged commitment to anti-semitism, each grounded in theological certainty; the façade of liberal pluralism hides an ingrained and 'scientifically' secure faith in racial segregation. Hubert's flight is a journey into the half-understood; he interprets familiar signs only to have his expectations shattered. For the reader this process is supplemented by Amis's darkly comic patchwork of recognizable names, practices and ideas which are no longer what we expect them to be.

In 'Four Fluent Fellows' (1973), an essay on *The Napoleon of Notting Hill*, Amis discloses the source of Chesterton's macabre stylistic experiment. Chesterton, he explains, is unlike Orwell or orthodox science fiction writers in that he does not attempt diagnoses or warnings about the nature of the contemporary world. Chesterton 'shows us, first, a society "almost exactly like what it is now", then, later, a creation of pure and free fancy'.[5] Amis in *The Alteration* does both, simultaneously. He seems to be arguing, and in his novel demonstrating, that the moral or ethical issues addressed by literature should draw the reader into its fictive design, but they should not instruct. Another essay, on Evelyn Waugh ('Fit to Kill', 1978), confirms this: 'No novel is a statement, and we should try to fight against making inferences about its author's state of mind'. He argues that in Waugh's later novels we cannot avoid these inferences, that he used his Catholicism to explain the imponderables and horrors of modern life and that his fiction reflected this desire for shape and security: 'We all know what Waugh found – to his artistic detriment'.[6] Amis was by no means an aesthete; he was disdainful of texts which self-consciously and in his view self-indulgently explored the boundaries of style. At the same time he refused to turn literature into a vehicle for a particular ideology or world view. His next experimental novel involves the opportunity to do both, but it manages to do neither.

Russian Hide-and-Seek (1980) is set in 2030, exactly fifty years after the publication of the novel and, within the novel, after

Britain's occupation by the Soviet Union. Some time around 2020 the Soviet empire had abandoned the Marxist version of feudalism and returned to its nineteenth-century incarnation. England in 2030 resembles those distant outposts of the tzarist monolith explored by the likes of Dostoyevksy, Tolstoy and Chekhov. History repeats itself. The title of the book refers to an elaborate version of the game played by pre-revolutionary Russian aristocrats, in which chance will determine whether the spun cylinder of a revolver comes to rest upon the live cartridge. The narrative centres upon the role of Alexander Petrovsky, a young cavalry officer drawn as much by boredom as idealism into the revolutionary activities of group 31. Unlike 1917, this revolution fails and the novel ends with Petrovsky's funeral.

Like *The Alteration, Russian Hide-and-Seek* scrupulously avoids prediction or diagnosis. Its parallels with the actual history of modern Europe are undermined by Amis's stylistic reframings. In chapter 2, two Russian bureaucrats greet one another with '*Good evening, my dear chap*' and '*Fine to see you, old customer*'. The dialogue is italicized because it is English, an inaccurate (*old customer* for example) but very fashionable revival of the lost culture of pre-occupation Britain. The English characters use the old language with a little more confidence and accuracy, and the effect of this device upon the reader is bizarre. The third-person account and most of the dialogue is rendered in convincingly modern English, but without Amis's usual locutionary range, ease and informality: it is a good translation, but like all translations it loses much of the original. This general sense of the novel as a refracted, imperfect version of what we might have had underpins its subplot: an attempt by the Russians to revive the English heritage with their 'New Cultural Programme'. If the novel has a message it is a version of the scepticism about art that we encounter in Amis's previous experimental writing: just as art should not attempt to impose meaning or order upon reality, so government-sponsored art programmes cannot make life or people any better than they were without them.

The novel ends with Kitty, Petrovsky's English lover, standing alone at his grave and half recalling some lines from an old English play that the Russians have revived.

something about somebody dying and being turned into stars and

34

put in the sky. With more concentration than she had ever summoned before, she tried to remember the precise words, just some of them, just one phrase, but she was not used to efforts of that kind. She tried again; she nearly got it. No. It was gone. (ch. 22)

Amis is playing a game with the reader's cultural antennae. Her lost reference is to Act III, scene 2 of *Romeo and Juliet*:

> when he shall die,
> Take him and cut him out in little stars
> And he will make the face of heaven so fine
> That all the world will be in love with night.

If we recognize her allusion we might feel mildly satisfied with our quiz-show competence, but what do we feel about Kitty's inability to remember the lines? Would they have provided her with some small comfort for her loss, a kind of cultural correlative enabling her to reschedule personal tragedy as high art?

The moment and the question are significant because they take us back to the middle of the novel, chapter 17, which involves the first performance of the revived play. It is attended, separately, by Alexander and Kitty, and the part of Juliet is played by Alexander's other occasional lover, Sarah Harland. The predominantly English audience does not enjoy the performance. They are bewildered by the arcane language and disappointed that the alleged archetype of pre-revolutionary English culture turns out to have written a play that is so irrelevant to life as they understand it. The performance is cut short by a fire, set by an unidentified arsonist, and the only fatality is Sarah. During the mayhem, Alexander has the opportunity to rescue her.

> From where he was it looked as if it might be too far. It just might be; that was enough. His decision must have shown in his face, because on to hers came a look of totally unsurprised contempt, a terrible look that was to haunt him till the day he died. He turned away to search for Kitty, for whom after all he was much more responsible.

Our feelings about his decision are not focused upon any insight into his feelings of shame or despair. This is not provided. Instead the entire episode involves a disturbing confrontation with the process by which emotion is filtered through a network of social and cultural reference points. We know that *Romeo and Juliet* draws together the most tragic

35

manifestations of love and death, and we are asked to compare our knowledge of Shakespeare's text with our ongoing experience of Amis's. Is Alexander's cold, pragmatic decision in any way influenced by the fact that he, like everyone else, inhabits a cultural wasteland? Is his behaviour symptomatic of the collective philistinism of the audience? Does cultural deprivation create a general state of moral and emotional nothingness? The novel certainly raises these questions but it offers no straightforward answers. The people of the novel, Russian and English, have become detached from the institutions and cultural benchmarks that enable us to organize our notions of morality and commitment: art, the church, society as a beneficent structure. We leave the novel still wondering if these elements of our lives reflect our innately good qualities or whether they sustain the fiction that such qualities can exist without them.

Ending Up (1974), published two years before *The Alteration*, is a hybrid. It involves an ostensibly realist frame of reference, but it adapts this to a structure that is at once appropriate and disconcerting. It takes us through the last three months in the lives of five septuagenarians who find themselves thrown together, by grim financial necessity, in a place called Tuppeny-Happeny Cottage. Muriel Spark's *Momento Mori* (1959), William Trevor's *The Old Boys* (1971) and John Bailey's *At the Jerusalem* (1967) constitute a subgenre of the elderly confinement novel and each injects an appropriate degree of compassionate good-humour into its largely conventional narrative. Amis, without cruelty, constructs a narrative that replicates the black comedy of ageing. Each chapter is rarely more than 1,500 words in length and through this strategy Amis achieves a multiplicity of effects. The narrative moves with alarming speed. We will encounter Bernard Bastable, the most disagreeable member of the group, arranging one of his bizarre and very cruel practical jokes and then the camera lens will take us upstairs to George Zeyer the mentally incapacitated ex-academic desperately trying to remember the right word. Within about four minutes of reading time we will join Marigold the ex-actress and Adela the spinsterish nobody in the woods near the cottage discussing Bernard's foul mannerisms. What actually happens is always interrupted or slowed

36

down by the incapacities and ingrained routines of the aged characters; but the reader feels that their story is accelerating, and in a horrible way it is. Everyone dies in the concluding chapter. They do so alone, in a variety of sordid and uncomfortable ways and none of them has the opportunity to reflect upon the death of anyone else. Their bodies are discovered by Bernard's son with whom he has not communicated for thirty years. The end has the grim textual symmetry of a Shakespearean fifth act and the entire text recalls the mixture of unreality and immediacy produced by Renaissance dramatic structure. Each brief chapter operates like a scene from a play and the overcrowded cottage, where the narrative occurs, is like the stage. The characters carry the entirety of their lives and memories into this compressed textual space, and as we leave it so do they, alone.

THE REALIST RETURNS: *JAKE'S THING* TO *THE BIOGRAPHER'S MOUSTACHE*

Through the 1960s and 1970s Amis alternated between one experimental novel and one which maintained the devices and contemporary focus of the fifties fiction. *I Want It Now* (1968) and *Girl 20* (1971) offer sceptical though not conservative views of 1960s culture and idealism. They recycle the satirical methods and narrational presences of the fifties material, with easier targets. This backward–forward exercise ended with *Russian Hide-and-Seek* (1980). After that the mixed-genre experiments ceased, and at the same time Amis began to infuse his realist techniques with a stylistic counterpattern that could be diagnosed as a mixture of indifference and contempt. This began with *Jake's Thing* (1978).

Jake's 'thing' is evidently his lack of desire to have sex with women. He is still able to, but he does not want to and he can't remember why he ever did. For Jake this condition is exaggerated by the fact that his prolific libidinous career was always a substantial part of everything else: his interest in sex was, it seems, coterminus with his interest in life. Jake's condition is not just the subject of the novel; it insinuates itself into all of the structural elements of the text.

The novel begins with a conversation between Jake and his GP about when Jake first noticed that 'something was wrong' and whether 'it' might be connected with the 'other trouble'. The opening is typically, almost self-consciously, Amisian. Before the third-person narrator tells us who the speakers are they might be discussing international politics or a car engine. Indeed, even after we are introduced to Jake Richardson and Dr Curnow their topic, Jake's sexual problem, remains undisclosed until chapter 2. The intervening passage, involving Jake's journey home to his wife Brenda, introduces us to a new and unprecedented departure in Amis's narrative method.

The plenitude of detail is obsessive and chaotic. We consider the practical and financial differences between taking a 127 bus or a taxi to Warren Street. We witness pedestrian lights, the Orris Park National Westminster Bank, double-parked cars with CD plates, a person Jake thinks he recognizes but who could well be the chap who played the superintendent in 'that police series', and road works with no one working on them. The narrator suggests a degree of distaste on Jake's part but we never pause for long enough to find out what Jake really thinks. Eventually Jake is enticed by the cut-price offers of Winesteads Ltd, and at the check-out he is obliged to listen to a man in 'dirty whitish overalls smoking a cigar and chatting to the senior of the two shopmen'.

> 'Is it worth it?' he asked a couple of times. 'This is it. If it isn't, I don't want to know. If it isn't, I'm not interested. If it is, then this is it. I mean, this is it. Right?'
> 'Right.'
> 'And it is. It bloody is. Like everything else.' As he talked the overalled man took a roll of £20 notes from his side pocket and counted some out; Jake thought five but wasn't sure. 'It bloody is. Twelve year old's better than '62. I mean, you know, this is it. Ever tried Jack Daniel's Green Label?'
> 'No.'
> 'Worth trying.' Change was handed over, not much. 'Ta. Yeah, worth trying. Shows you the Black's worth it. Green's good though. Well, cheers.'
> 'Cheers.'

The passage functions as a perfect denouement for Jake's trek through featureless London. The opening speech carries echoes of Pinter and Beckett, and this disquisition on the enigmatic significance of 'it' tapers into the loud banality of the price of whisky. If we had read any Amis fiction before this, we would expect the narrator to offer us Jake's sardonic reflections on this scene; how it presents a darkly comic confirmation of his feelings of dissatisfaction with contemporary life, even its mildly surreal echoes of his own conversation with Dr Curnow. What happens is that Jake becomes engaged in a rather sad exchange on whether the ten per cent discount also covers the chocolates he has bought for his wife. 'Jake paid, picked up his goods and left, remembering he should have said Cheers as the exit door swung shut after him. Out on the street he noticed that away from the sunlight the air was chilly.'

Jake Richardson is Jim Dixon thirty-five years older. There are plenty of intertextual clues: Jim, James, Jake; Dixon, Richardson, Dickson. Unlike Jim, Jake has stayed in the academic profession; his specialization is, appropriately, more ancient than Jim's, and his interest in his subject has become, as Jim's already was, little more than a dutiful habit. But these are red herrings. Jake's most significant relationship with Jim involves his difference from him as a literary device. Jim's inner world would have exacted a farcical revenge upon the terrible bore in the whitish overalls. Jake's inner world is more concerned with the price of the chocolates. *Jake's Thing*, as the above passage demonstrates, is a darkly comic novel, but the comedy is made available to the reader via the narrator. Jake, we assume, sees it too, but he does not comment on it or distance himself from it. It is part of his own bleak condition.

Just as John Lewis in *That Uncertain Feeling* (1955) carried characteristics of Jim Dixon into his first-person account, so Stanley Duke of *Stanley and the Women* (1984) is Jake Richardson telling his own story. His story is not too different; it involves Stanley's inability to understand the women with whom he is or has been involved. Jake consults a psychoanalyst as a cure for his sexual problems; Stanley's psychotic son, Steve, is referred to two psychoanalysts, whose different methods are equally ineffective.

When faced with a variety of imponderable and tangible disasters Amis's characters had previously taken control of their fictional context. Whether they were working alongside their narrator or speaking directly to the reader, they reconstituted, reorganized their situation often with the consoling dimension of dark humour. Stanley, like Jake, is different; he is confused and, as a narrator, genuinely, rather than cleverly or wittily, unreliable. He discloses the details of his life with almost embarrassing candour, but he makes no real attempt to understand them.

The opening pages of the novel comprise a detailed and by no means critical description of his current wife, Susan, her career, her personal history, and their house, in which a dinner party is taking place. Only after about a thousand words do we realize that the person telling the story exists in it. This anxious reticence and absence of any clear point of focus sets the tone for the rest of the book. Later, Stanley delivers a verbatim report of a conversation between Susan, a literary critic, and Nash, one of the psychoanalysts, involving the medical, ethical, philosophical and creative dimensions of madness. He exists on the margins and he does not offer the reader his opinion on their ideas. At other times he addresses the reader as he would a friend, carelessly digressing, losing narrative focus in subclauses that collect apparently irrelevant scraps of information. This is his description of the few minutes he spends with his son just before Steve is admitted to a mental home.

> Those last few words of Steve's turned out to be very easy to remember. They stayed around while I watched him silently – except for eating noises – get through a couple of bowls of soup and some ham and some bread in the kitchen, and incidently while Nash sat on in the sitting room and wrote a lot of stuff for the hospital and ate Brie and cream crackers and drank a glass of red wine, just what he had ordered actually, though without specifying the rather pricey Burgundy that, feeling a bit of a coward, I had opened for him.

These verbal wanderings are plausible in that Stanley is telling a story that he wishes had not happened. Just as he avoids lengthy reflections on the significance of Nash's and Susan's conversation so he continually reroutes his own emotional unease via his self-consciously irrelevant interest in food and drink.

In the experiments, Amis had used fiction to cloud the boundaries between the tangibly plausible and the unreal. These novels were his creative mission statement: despite its superhuman frame of reference the novel should not be used as an attempt to explain our non-fictional experience. In *Jake's Thing* and *Stanley and the Women*, Amis enacts these principles in texts that play by the rules of realist plausibility. It is left to the reader to sympathize with Stanley or feel contempt for his indifferent, unfocused emotional state. He does not help us with this decision; indeed, he virtually compels us to make the kind of judgements we would normally reserve for the non-fictional world. Jake too prompts an open verdict. We might be amused, even consoled, by the darkly comic framework of his journey home, but he isn't, and the narrator arranges the account to leave us with an uneasy choice. Should we laugh or cry?

After *Stanley and the Women* Amis began his final stage of stylistic recycling: everything from Jim Dixon to Stanley Duke resurfaces, but the last novels are by no means lazy or ineffective; quite the contrary.

In his Booker Prize winner, *The Old Devils* (1986), he plays a joke with himself and his readers. The plot focuses upon Alun Weaver, who was once Alan. The change of letter is part of his ruthless exploitation of his Welsh origins. He is a media Welshman, who has returned to his Celtic home to write a novel based on the life and works of one Brydan, the poet with no Christian name who is clearly Dylan Thomas. Alun is a catalyst. Each chapter carries the name of one of the characters with whom, in his earlier years, he has had affairs and arguments, inspired love, contempt and grudging respect. All of them have inherited features of male and female figures from Amis's fifties fiction, around the time when they all first knew Alun.

Consider the following. Amis's earliest creations have entered late middle age and they have taken their narrators with them. The interchanges between their public, spoken presences and their inner reflections maintain their original qualities of crafted, sardonic irony, but this is less anxious; ease has replaced provocation. The exception is Alun. He is a combination of Jim Dixon, John Lewis, Garnet Bowen and Roger Micheldene. The disruptive energy that had been visited upon the fifties reader now returns, undimmed, to the fictional and more comfortable lives of Alun's fifties companions.

In chapter 3 the focus is upon Charlie, and he looks on as Alun mocks, jokes and humiliates his way through a series of social encounters. At one point Alun deals with Llywelyn

41

Caswallon Pugh, an official of the Cymric Companionship of the USA, by exposing, without explicitly ridiculing, the absurdities of his obsessive Pennsylvanian Welshness. Charlie observes:

> The fluid, seamless way Alun converted his unthinking glance towards the waiting car into an urgent request for assistance for somebody to accompany his Mr Pugh, was something that Charlie was quite sure he would never forget... At the moment before he ducked his head under the car roof Charlie caught a last glimpse of Pugh, looking not totally unlike an inflated rubber figure out of whose base the stopper had been drawn an instant earlier. Charlie might have felt some pity had he not been lost in admiration for Alun.
> 'Bloody marvellous bit of timing,' he told him as they were settled in the back seats.

Charlie here is like a reader of *Lucky Jim* who returns to it thirty years later and is still impressed by Jim's and his narrator's ability to cunningly ridicule those aspects of life that we might otherwise tolerate.

Amis's folding of the non-fictional into the fictional has a punch line. Alun dies of a heart-attack. The stylistic energy that Alun had injected into the fictional lives of his peers gradually diminishes, but, with grim irony, they become happier people. They settle their differences, and achieve a level of honesty that they had previously, for some reason, denied themselves.

The death of Alun is rather like the departure of Prospero from his island. In his last four novels Amis never again offers us a character who exerts the same level of control over his own fictional world.

In *Difficulties with Girls* (1988) we find Patrick and Jenny of *Take a Girl Like You* married and in a state of relative happiness. It is 1967 and Amis is reworking the double-focus narrative of the first novel with the benefit of twenty years' hindsight on what men and women were really like in the 1960s. The intriguing relationship between these two novels will be dealt with in the next chapter.

The Russian Girl (1992) presents us with Dr Richard Vaisey, a lecturer in Slavonic Studies, and Anna, a visiting Russian poet. When planning the novel, Amis must have had in mind an incident that had occurred three decades before, and which he records in the essay 'Kipling Good'.[7] In 1962, while still a Fellow of Peterhouse, Cambridge, Amis hosted a visit and reading by the Russian poet Yevtushenko. Amis's record of their conversation centres upon Yevtushenko asking him what he thinks of *Dr Zhivago*. Amis states that he has not read it because 'an interest in the paraphrasable content of literature [is] an anti-literary interest' (p. 170). *The Russian Girl* begins with a re-run of the same conversation. This time Richard's head of department, Hallett, is trying to persuade him that it would be better for students to read Dostoyevsky's *Crime and Punishment* in English than not at all. Richard will not be moved. 'You know as well as I do that every word Dostoyevsky writes is written in a way only he can write it. A translation, even the best imaginable, has got to leave all that out'. This theme of the relationship between literary language, indeed all language, and its paraphrasable content is the enduring subtext of the novel.

Richard falls in love with Anna Danilova, completely. His attraction to her parallels his commitment to literature. He knows Russian almost as well as he knows English, and his appreciation of the literary forms that feed on both languages allows him a kind of literary adultery: two separate lives, contacts and intimate acts of communication. Anna is the sexual and emotional personification of everything that has involved his intellect: he can talk to her in Russian and English, she is beautiful and she writes poetry.

Described as such the novel sounds like the kind of middle-brow love story with which one would not expect Amis, the hardened cynic, to be associated. The book is rescued from the cosy satisfactions of this subgenre by its cunning, almost self-referential, use of disclosures and blind spots. At Anna's first public reading Richard is reduced to tears. 'He wept that all that honesty of feeling, which he could not doubt it was, all that seriousness of purpose, all that sincerity...should have come to nothing'. In his view, she is a stylistic failure, and it is at this point that Richard's opening remarks on what translation can only leave out begin to fold into the narrative, in a very disorientating manner. We can neither agree nor disagree with Richard's evaluation. We trust the content of his emotional response, but we remain unaware of the actuality of the words and their effect upon him that give it shape: it is 'translated'. At the end of the reading Anna and Richard know, and we know, that they have fallen in love. The episode is like a rerun of James's and Catherine's almost wordless shift from brief acquaintance to total commitment in *The Anti-Death League*. But in *The Russian Girl* the inexpressible is transformed into the equally mysterious process of distilling irreducible truth from layers of language. She asks him if he thought her poems were good.

> 'What can I say? Before it was over I was in floods of tears. Not much poetry makes me cry. I tried not to let you see. I felt...'

The narrator comments that 'Anna believed what he had said, had taken it for the truth, which it was, and what he could not have said was that it was not the truth that she took it for'.

Richard's lie that is not a lie continues to trouble him. He leaves his wife and commits himself to Anna, but he is unable to lay to rest the feeling that he cannot really be in love if he is so unsettled by the stylistic quality of his lover's poetry. At the end of the novel Anna gives him a poem, in Russian, about their relationship, and after he has read it she tells him that she knew what he was really thinking after her public reading. 'But that lie told me how much you loved me, and it means I'll always love you. I don't think I could put that into a poem'. In short, what they feel is untranslatable. The notion that love cannot be described might seem like high romantic waffle, were it not for the fact that our experience of reading the novel involves a tantalizing encounter with something that is tangibly present but which always disappears into the gaps between the discourses.

The last poem is offered to us, but, as the narrator explains, it is an English translation that appeared a year later. It is a sincere, unambiguous assembly of clichés, banal metaphors and verbal repetitions. Or so we think, until we remember Richard's opening remarks on what happens when Russian literature is read in English: 'A what? A pale – distorted – shrivelled ghost of the reality'. The English version might justify Richard's evaluation of the stylistic quality of the original, but what does it leave out? This question rolls back through the narrative. Sometimes they speak in Russian. The narrator tells us this but he never tells us what they say. Significantly, when they are alone after the public reading and after Anna shows him her latest poem the narrator does not tell us whether they are speaking English or Russian, and the locative verbal clues that sometimes identify Anna's English are absent. The question of what we might have lost is here particularly intriguing, and it attends our reading of the entire novel. Anna and Richard are drawn to each other in a way that transcends their mutual physical attraction; we know this, but the exact nature of their emotional intimacy is always deferred, never defined or explained. The narrator offers us versions of what happens, but as Richard has told us, 'A translation, even the best imaginable, has got to leave all that out.'

It is an impressively multi-layered novel. The parallels between Richard's commitment to literature and his love for Anna; the narrator's use of signposts to shifts between Russian and English, and his removal of them at crucial points; the perplexing question of what her poems are really like, of whether they tell us something more about her; the sense of having heard some of the things they say to each other, but not all; the frequent references to the unreliability of translation – all of these contribute to a book and an effect that Amis, except in his poetry, had never attempted before or after *The Russian Girl*. It is a shameless celebration of something – love – that it cannot describe.

All of Amis's novels have carried traces of autobiography. The appalling Margaret Peel of *Lucky Jim* is based, partly, on Amis's first meetings with Philip Larkin's life-long girlfriend–companion Monica Jones (full name: Margaret Monica Beale Jones). Neddy Welch's obsessive interest in folk culture echoes the similar, and in Amis's view similarly loathsome, enthusiasms of his then father-in-law, Leonard Bardwell. *Jake's Thing* and *Stanley and the Women* incorporate elements of his own experiences of lost sex-drive and marital breakdown. But most of these intersections between life and work are relevant only to the reader with particular interests in the former. Our knowledge of which parts of the novels correspond with real events, people and experiences will not alter the fact that Amis's skill exists in his ability to turn the fabric of the novel into another world. Margaret Peel's resemblance to Monica Jones is of minor significance compared with Margaret Peel's function in the mind and life of Jim Dixon.

In a number of the 1990s novels the autobiographical parallels became more linear and dependable. The actuality of his own life, its circumstances, conditions, indeed its narrative, became a mirror of its fictional counterpart. In *The Folks That Live on the Hill* (1990) the central character, Harry Caldecote, is retired, twice married and spends a good deal of his time in the King's public house and in the Irving, a decent London club. Amis by this time had moved into the upper storey of a house in Primrose Hill, the downstairs part of which was occupied by his first wife Hilly and her third husband Alastair Boyd, Lord Kilmarnock. Amis, like Harry, drank in the local pub, the Queen's, and spent afternoons at his club, the Garrick. Also, like Harry, his social existence was comprised largely of people from his previous lives – friends, relatives, ex-wives. The autobiographical parallels are continuous and largely innocuous. Amis seems to be inviting anyone who knows anything about him to follow the clues – but there are no revelations. The novel tells us no more about the private world of Kingsley Amis than do any of his previous fictional characters or Amis himself in his *Memoirs* and essays. The most significant and enduring feature of the book is its peculiar style. Harry is the central character, but the third-person narrator carries us into the lives of his niece Fiona, his 'ex-stepdaughter' Bunty, his sister Clare and his brother Freddie. Yet Harry is never completely absent. His own relationship with the narrator involves a clever facsimile of old age.

The first three pages of chapter 13 tell us about Harry having his hair cut. For about 500 words there is no dialogue. We follow the random, largely disinterested thoughts of Harry on age and hair, and things he has recently read about the influence of Mrs Thatcher upon the hairdressing unions. Suddenly he sees in the mirror an image of his brother Freddie's face counterposed with his own, and we are invited to interpret this as a symptom of unfocused, regressive senility. But it is not. His brother is there, sitting behind him, and Harry, with shameless glee, visits upon Freddie the experience that we think he has just had. He surprises him. 'Probably no human being has ever shied so much like a startled horse, especially from a seated, even slumped posture, but anyone who saw Freddie just then must have been forgiven for thinking along such lines.'

This episode is interesting because it offers us a third version of Jim Dixon. The second, Jake Richardson, had cut himself off from the cunning strategies of his narrator. Harry and Harry's narrator co-operate in a way that verges upon the postmodern.

When we enter the world of Fiona, Clare or Freddie, we know that the sardonic, mildly intimate relationship between ourselves, Harry and the narrator goes with us. The joke that Harry and the narrator play on Freddie takes us into Freddie's world through Harry's and his narrator's eyes. And when Harry is removed from the experiences of his friends and relatives we feel that he is still there, as if he, or his alter-ego the narrator, is showing them to us again through Harry's eyes. Everything that they do, all of their personal experiences and encounters will at some point involve a reference to their relationship with Harry.

No one really does anything of great significance or goes anywhere or nurtures grand ambitions. (Harry is offered a comfortable post-retirement job as a librarian in America, but he rejects it.) Instead they constantly look back to what they have done and how this affects their current condition. We begin to wonder why these characters, who are not all as old as Harry, seem to be so like Harry. They are like Harry because just as Jim Dixon and his narrator made a very dull world exciting so Harry Caldecote and his narrator show us the world as he sees it: moribund, repetitive, but rather amusing. In *Ending Up* (1974) Amis had explored the potential horrors of getting old from the relatively safe distance of middle age. *The Folks That Live on the Hill*, written almost two decades later, is far more optimistic.

You Can't Do Both (1994) is Amis's most autobiographical novel. We follow Robin Davies from his adolescence in pre-war south London, through Oxford during the war, to an eventual readership in a provincial university. The fact that Robin's family, unlike Amis's, is Welsh and that significant parts of the novel take place during his visits to Wales is not a red herring. Amis's life as academic, novelist, poet and family man effectively began in Wales, and outside London Wales was the only place where he ever felt at home. But the novel is far more personal than even these narrative parallels suggest. Its subject is Robin's attitude to love and sex. The 'both' that his father and wife tell him that he can't do is to have a family life with the woman he tells himself that he loves, and sex with practically every other woman who is attracted to him. He does do both, and the novel ends with Nancy, his enduring partner, giving him a black eye in the hotel room he has reserved for another of his incessant acts of betrayal.

In order to fully appreciate the novel the reader must either be addicted to Amis's fiction or be part of his life. In the former case you will recognize in Robin the temperamental and behavioural characteristics of practically all of Amis's male characters. Robin is lecherous, charming, intelligent, unfixed and prone to reflections upon his failings. But he is unlike any of his predecessors because he is unnervingly transparent. There are no layers of farce, self parody, wit, sardonic reflection, or narrative excursion to protect Robin from a full disclosure of his predicament. Amis shows us the life that provided the narratives of Jim Dixon, John Lewis, Garnet Bowen, Patrick Standish, Roger Micheldene *et al.*, but without their fictional personae. Robin is Amis, and Nancy is Hilly, his first wife. The novel's style, so unlike anything he had ever written before, is an act of confession, to Hilly.

Amis's last novel, *The Biographer's Moustache* (1995), is an intriguing blend of mirrors, false clues and blind alleys. It was published in the same year, 1995, that Eric Jacobs published his biography of Amis. Over the previous two and a half years Jacobs had spent several days a week drinking, dining and talking with Amis. In the diary that Jacobs published in the *Sunday Times* soon after Amis's death, their relationship, at least in Jacob's view, resembled a modern version of Boswell and Johnson. During the same period Amis had published *You Can't Do Both*, his most candid, though fictionalized, account of his own life. His last novel, involving the relationship between a journalist and his biographical subject, an elderly novelist, would seem to be founded upon immediate experience. Yet these tantalizing similarities between the fictional and the actual are superficial. The novel is effectively an act of expurgation. Amis systematically excises any connections between our knowledge of his world and the story of the biographer and the novelist. The fact that he supplies the former, Gordon Scott Thompson, with an intrusive middle name and the latter, J. R. P. Fane, with the familar title of 'Jimmie' is probably his last false trail for truffle-hunting scholars. Jacobs is indeed a 'Scot'; and 'Jim' Dixon was part of the Amis mythology that he was never 'fain' to disregard.

Fane is a Bloomsbury Group throwback, in love with the pure aesthetics and psychological intensities of literary creation, and even more closely attached to the habits and prejudices of the

English aristocracy. He is everything that Amis is not. Gordon hates his novels, which seem to have attained a minor cult status among devotees of self-indulgent inaccessibility, and he eventually comes to detest their author. Jacobs praised Amis's novels because they are nothing like this, and his biography involved an inexhaustible admiration for Amis.

Fane has agreed to participate in the biography, but he turns each interview into a mixture of avoidance and incitement. Gordon's enquiries regarding his opinions are subtly transformed by Fane into investigations of Gordon's own ambitions, social class, temperament and intentions regarding Fane's wife Joanna. The reader is left with the impression that the only good novel that Fane might have written is the one that he has strenuously avoided; in which the manipulative verbal skills, the opportunistic nastiness of J. R. P. Fane are offered to the central character.

When discussing the biography with his publisher, Gordon concedes that it will sell not because Fane is a literary cult figure but because his life intersects with the fantastic indulgences of the English upper classes. He knows that its claim to be a 'literary life' is a token gesture, a fraudulent concession to respectability. At the end of the book, Gordon abandons the biography. He tells both his publisher and Fane that he cannot involve himself in a text whose subject he finds so repulsive. We know he is lying. He has had an affair with Fane's wife Joanna, and his attraction to her is more than physical. His real reason for abandoning his Life of Fane is that it has become part of his own.

Amis's last novel is a beautifully crafted exercise in the ironies of fabrication. The novel about Fane tells us more than the biography ever could, and the biographer does not need to produce a fascinating insight into his mysterious subject because, by existing in the novel, he has already done so. The other presence who leads us confidently through this maze of real lives and written lives, fiction and non-fiction, is of course the narrator. And who is he? He is the Kingsley Amis that most of us know but have never met. He is the figure who, since *Lucky Jim*, has constructed, orchestrated and introduced us to worlds that soon became as familiar as our own. As a person, he is a shadowy presence; as an experience he is a fitting memorial to the man who cast the shadow.

SHORT STORIES

Amis's Introduction to his *Collected Short Stories* (1980) opens with a discussion of what short stories are and why people read them. Amis hates the modern tendency to turn the form into 'the impression, the untrimmed slice of life, the landscape with figures but without characters' (p. 10). This trend, he feels, has been promoted by the kind of periodical 'subsidized by the Arts Council' which does not care too much about pleasing the public. Consequently, 'the term "short story" has become a fully fledged consumer-deterrent in its own right, like "sensitive study" in a different context' (p. 11). Amis, citing Kipling as a precedent, holds that the short story should be a distilled novel, involving a narrative that holds our attention, characters that we get to know and a situation that invites us in.

His own short stories satisfy these criteria. His realist stories are as Amis puts it 'chips from a novelist's work bench'. They enable him to re-explore themes which, for whatever reason, exist only in the margins of his realist novels. In 'Moral Fibre', John Lewis of *That Uncertain Feeling* returns, this time as a witness to events outside his own world of uncertainties. The story tells us little more about Lewis than we already know, but he becomes more of a channel for Amis's growing scepticism with political and social diagnosis. Mair Webster, a social worker, is the principal target. She regards the mildly criminal, promiscuous and irresponsible Betty as a symptom of social inequality and a poor education system; Lewis and Amis regard her as rather like anyone else who wants to have a good time. 'I Spy Strangers' was written in 1962 but takes us back to Amis's army experience. It is Germany in 1945 just before the massive Labour victory in the first post-war general election. The tensions, anticipations and anxieties that attended the new government and all it promised are played out among the officers and men of a Royal Corps of Signals company. It is Britain in miniature, a collection of people attempting to reinvent themselves, and it is a mildly engaging mess.

Far more intriguing are the stories in which the genre-mixing, plausibility-testing features of his experimental novels are projected into writing which almost defies categorization. His experimental novels test the boundaries between the credible and the blatantly unreal, and their short-story counterparts are at once commentaries on and extreme versions of this procedure. Amis betrays a special concern with these pieces by devoting the second half of his Introduction to a discussion of one of them: 'Who or What Was It?' His account is uneasy and perplexed. It comes close to being his creative manifesto, but it can only be properly understood if read as a kind of Swiftian footnote to the stories themselves.

'Who or What Was It?' was originally a radio script, read by Amis himself, and which, he explains, seems to have had a similar effect to Orson Welles's 1938 reading of his near namesake's *The War of the Worlds*. In 1938 thousands of Americans besieged bus terminals, fled along streets and drove off into the countryside because they believed that Martians had landed. Nothing like this happened in Britain but Amis was, after the broadcast, besieged by enquiries. His old friend, the novelist Bruce Montgomery, telephoned to ask if the story was true. A TV producer phoned to ask if it could be used in a new series of programmes on the supernatural, suggesting that they might take cameras along to the actual location. And an academic from the Religious Experience Research Unit at Manchester College, Oxford, wrote to Amis that it was intriguingly unlike any of the supernatural-religious experiences they had so far recorded.

'Who or What Was It?' is 'about' Amis's novel *The Green Man*. Amis and his wife Elizabeth Jane Howard come across a pub of the same name, though in not quite the same area, owned by one Maurice Allington. The 'coincidences' multiply to the extent that Amis and Jane decide to phone Bob Conquest to ask him to drive up as a third witness. No answer. They try Jane's brother Colin ('Monkey'), who is at a party, and Amis's son Philip, who doesn't have the use of a car. The story is so crowded with personal detail that we begin to wonder what kind of joke Amis is playing. There are references to habits, tastes and idiosyncrasies that only an acquaintance or an obsessive fan could verify as characteristics of the real Amis. (They are all authentic.)

Amis eventually encounters the supernatural beast of his novel. Jane has lent him a gold cross – her grandmother's – which she wears around her neck. He throws it at the beast and the thing–apparition disappears. The twist in the tale occurs

51

when he returns to their room. Jane is surprised, since Amis had already been back once, returned the cross and spent some time with his wife. Later she tells him that he, or whoever it was, had got into bed with her, and that she has been to see their GP.

> It was negative, then, I said. Yes, Jane said.
> Well, that's it. A relief, of course. But in one way, rather disappointing. (p. 225)

It is an occasional habit of fiction writers to break down the boundaries between their own and their fictional worlds, but none as far as I know has caused one of his created presences, and in this case an agent of Satan, to have unprotected sex with his wife.

The story becomes even more intriguing when we compare it with Amis's almost obsessive account in his Introduction of its consequences.

> My intention had been to fool listeners into thinking it was a factual account until three quarters of the way through and then, with luck, induce them to suspend their altogether necessary disbelief for the last few minutes. The detail about the cross was put in partly to make incredulity inescapable and final. For some, it missed its mark most grievously. (p. 11)

Amis seems to be perplexed by his own ability to make the blatantly implausible believable, but his unease runs deeper than this and causes him, briefly, to uncover his own emotional and intellectual concerns.

> All sorts of people are uncomfortable in a universe where there seems to be nothing supernatural, nothing beyond this life, no undiscovered forces, no God. I sympathize; I find it none too cosy myself; but I do wish there were a little less eager, cruising credulity about. I wish too, quite vainly, that such people, other people too, would face a little more squarely what is entailed by believing, or believing in, something. (p. 12)

This is as close as Amis ever came to showing us what might lie behind his agnostic, sceptical presence. The statement is obtuse and by his normal standards enigmatic, but its meaning turns on his use of the word 'believing'. Belief in anything beyond the logical, the empirical and the tangible was, for Amis, an impossible but necessary human aspiration. He resolved this paradox in his addiction, as writer and reader, to fiction. Fiction can offer us the emotional and spiritual satisfactions of a not quite parallel universe, a world in which our familiar expectations and responses become intertwined with experiences that, for a short time, we have to believe. This is why he became so annoyed with those people who continued to suspend disbelief: for Amis the reading of fiction as reality was as bad as living permanently in a world of fictions and fantasies.

Amis gave particular attention to 'Who or What Was It?' because a number of his other short stories offer similarly disturbing confluences between the real and the created unreal.

'The Darkwater Hall Mystery' is, superficially, a light-hearted exercise in pastiche. It is a Sherlock Holmes story, but, due to his partner's temporary indisposition, Watson is in complete control. Watson's meticulous formality of style is reproduced to the extent that he is largely indistinguishable from Conan Doyle's creation – but not quite. He discloses at the end of the story that when Dolores, the beautiful wife of the butler, offered him the vital, case-solving piece of information, they were in bed together. It must have occurred to most late-twentieth century readers that their knowledge of Victorians is two-dimensional. In literature we read through the institutionalized mannerisms of contemporary style and reassemble the presence behind the words. But, given the frozen conventions of the period, much is left to our imagination. Amis causes the imagined and the fictive presence to inhabit the same text.

'To See the Sun' is set in 1925 and involves letters from Stephen Hillier to his wife, Connie, and his Oxford colleague and friend, A. C. Winterbourne. Hillier writes these from an obscure part of the Balkans where he is investigating local folklore and literature. Our other perspective on the events behind the letters is provided by the private journal of Countess Valvazour, Hillier's host. We learn from this that she and Hillier have had an affair and that although she looks and behaves like a 29-year-old she is in fact 150, and a vampire. Again Amis is playing a game with credulity and disbelief. Hillier's letters are paradigms of period style and non-disclosure. He suggests to his friend that something improper and disturbing has occurred, and he keeps everything from his wife. Amis might have used the epistolary form to emphasize only the deceptions of adultery, with the reader as the focus for this nexus of truth and lies: we alone see the Countess's journal. But instead he makes us become participants in the process of deception. In his final letter to his wife, Hillier makes fun of the folklore of vampirism and related tales of the supernatural: they are myths built on myths, an edifice secured by the very English taste for the gothic. His letter could be a real document in that he employs the same idiom of easy assurance both to dismiss the folk myth of vampirism and to cover his adulterous tracks. And when we read it, the double lie maintained by Hillier causes a similarly double-edged sense of unease in our dealings with the story. At one level our suspension of disbelief enables us to engage with the social and stylistic elements that unite Hillier, Winterbourne and Connie: he could easily be lying to his wife about a very ordinary affair or confiding in his friend about an etherially romantic adventure in the Balkans. At another we read through his letters to the Countess's journal, to a fictional subtext which in itself defies credibility and dismantles the fabric of credibility that Hillier builds into his letters, which constitute the remainder of the text. The effect is similar to that of Maurice Allington's account of his meeting with God: he is a wonderfully believable presence and we cannot believe in him without believing his story. But in 'To See the Sun' the reader is placed in an even more difficult position by being obliged to witness separate textual components of the same narrative. In the Countess's journal she gives an account of them in her chamber, fantasizing as illicit lovers about how she might return with him to England, 'go to London and see the churches and the palaces and the people, and we walk in the park and sail on the river'. At one level their exchange causes us to speculate beyond the words to their hypothetical context, as we do with all traumatic moments in fictional relationships: will Hillier separate from Connie? will the Countess lead a secret life as the other woman? is it an impractical fantasy? But again we have to draw back from our transposition of real and fictional layers, because we know not only that the Countess will never visit London with Hillier but that she, and consequently he, could never have existed at all in any rational, plausible world.

The story is not simply an exercise in credulity twisting. It explores the conditions and circumstances of deception in a manner that only fiction can achieve. If Hillier's affair with the Countess had been only that, it would have remained a secret, a part of his life to which only he had access; to everyone else in the story it would never have existed. In a curious and ingenious way Amis recreates this same disjunction between the actual and the unknown in our encounter with the text: we get to know Stephen Hillier and the Countess, but in the process we must accept that they can never by the remotest possibility have existed. It recalls Amis's request that we 'face a little more squarely what is entailed by believing, or believing in, something'.

'The House on the Headland' is a story within a story, the former consisting of an account by Robert Chalmers of events that had occurred on Crete forty years earlier in 1899. This he assembles from a set of files passed on to him by a colleague in the Foreign Office. They involve the practices of one Count Alex who apparently has had procreative sex with women with two heads, three legs and in one case the face of a dog. For us the story is unbelievable, but not for Chalmers. He was born somewhere in the eastern Mediterranean in the same year, and adopted by a British diplomat. He has a reasonably innocent taste for the literary macabre and bizarre, and he also has a scar on his hip that has always made him suspect that he is a twin. The year is 1939, and at the end of his tale Chalmers decides to leave the Foreign Office, join the regular army and break off his engagement with Celia. A note at the end tells us that he died in action 'when showing complete disregard for his own safety'.

The story of Count Alex defies credibility, but Chalmers believes it; moreover, he believes that he is part of it. This is 1939. Something terrible is about to happen, but the inhuman depths of the horror would not be fully disclosed until after it had occurred. Amis wrote the story in 1979, like Chalmers forty years after a series of events that he now knows are true but which resist our attempts to reconcile what happened with our rationale of the human condition.

Amis's collection concludes with a very short story called 'Mason's Life'. Mason is approached in a pub by a man called Pettigrew who informs him that he, Mason, does not exist, that he is part of Pettigrew's dream. At the end Pettigrew tells him that he can hear the bedside telephone, that he is waking up. Mason grabs Pettigrew's arm and watches his own hand disappear. What makes the story particularly disturbing is Amis's placing of Mason, not Pettigrew, at the point of intersection between the third-person narrative and the dialogue. It is, recalling Amis's other narrator–character alliances, Mason's text. And when it ends, so does he. We, the readers, only know Pettigrew from what he says and what the narrator tells us he looks like, but we empathize with Mason. We suspend disbelief; we believe that Pettigrew is the liar.

We see the fictional world through Mason's eyes, but Pettigrew reminds us of Amis's comment that, in fiction, incredulity is eventually 'inescapable and final'.

3

Sex

An intriguing story attends the publication of *Stanley and the Women* (1984). It could not find a publisher in the United States and the *Times Literary Supplement*'s American correspondent supplies an account. 'I shall state the obvious and say that there are influential feminists who believe that the reading public should be spared certain fictions...three [of the potential publishers] candidly excused the rescinding of such offers by reference to objections from feminists on the editorial board' (*TLS*, 'American Notes', November 1984). The novel eventually found a home with an imprint of Simon and Schuster.

The *TLS* report is partly speculation, but it is underpinned by the fact that Amis's usual American publishers were reluctant to take on a book that many reviewers found to be an outright celebration of misogyny. In 1984 the women's movement had become an active constituent of literary criticism, an association begun with books such as Kate Millett's *Sexual Politics* (1970). Millett argued that male authors, specifically Lawrence, Miller, Mailer and Genet, had in their representation of male and female characters reproduced the normative values and expectations of a patriarchal society. Millett did not suggest that their works should be banned or ignored; rather that the reader should respect the literary credentials of the author while recognizing that these carry the ideological burden of male assumptions, prejudices and fantasies. John Carey suggests that with Amis's novel this is an impossible ideal.

> If you are a middle-aged chauvinist alcoholic you will enjoy this novel, and its narrator Stanley Duke will strike you as a perfectly normal and reliable chap. If you are any other kind of reader, you will be assailed by doubts. Does Kingsley Amis mean you to notice what a deadly specimen of humankind Stanley is? Does he notice it himself? If so, how can he expect you to swallow Stanley's version of

events, as the novel seems to count on you doing?[1]

According to Millett, good literature cannot alter the prejudices and inequalities of the society which formed its (male) author and from which it draws its material. According to Carey, Amis has written a novel which deliberately and calculatingly promotes the worst features of this society. Consequently, it should not be treated as literature but as a malicious polemic which exploits its literary vehicle. Is Stanley a cipher for Amis's chauvinistic nastiness? If he is not, then what is he?

Stanley's current wife, Susan, is a broadsheet literary editor, a liberal, sophisticated woman who is tolerant of Stanley's idiosyncrasies and supportive in his problems with Steve, his psychotic son. At least she is until she pretends that Steven has knifed her: she really wants him committed to the madhouse, out of the way. Nowell, his ex-wife and Steven's mother, travels miles across London to Stanley's house after hearing of Steve's breakdown. But in their interview with the psychoanalyst, she seems almost to rejoice in Dr Collings's thesis that Stanley is the principal cause of his son's madness. Trish Collings turns the screw. She is a feminist devotee of R. D. Laing and insists that Steve's 'cure' must involve him in a regressive confrontation with the worst aspects of his condition. What she also wants is the humiliation of Stanley: he must accept that he has ruined Steve, that he didn't really want the child, that his insistence that the teenage Steve should pass exams, succeed and get a job is a version of his own dependence upon male aggression. And, according to Nowell, Trish hates Stanley because she fancies him.

These women are horrible individuals, but are they horrible because they are women? Most of the men are no better. Cliff, Jake's colleague and drinking partner, is enthusiastic about the recently disclosed trend in wife battering. Bert, Nowell's current husband, gets drunk and frequently pretends to be drunk to avoid conversations with Nowell: 'who could like her after they got to know her, after they'd seen her in action?' Nash, the other psychoanalyst, regards madness as a clinical condition, not curable by Collings's Laingian strategies nor for that matter by much else. He regards women as one of the causes of male madness because 'they're all too monstrously, sickeningly, *terrifyingly* sane. That's the *whole trouble*'. The men of the novel are just as disagreeable as the women, but Stanley chooses the

58

women as the target for his final, aggressive diatribe.

> 'The root of the trouble', I said, 'is we want to fuck them, the pretty ones, women I mean . . . In fact women only want one thing, for men to want to fuck them. If they do, it means that they can fuck them up. Am I drunk? What was I trying to say, if you want to fuck a woman she can fuck you up. And if you don't want to she fucks you up anyway for not wanting to . . . that's what Women's Lib is for'. (ch. 4)

As a narrator, Stanley records the opinions of other people about sex, relationships and madness. He doesn't comment on them; instead his narrative exposes their various states of hypocrisy, uselessness and dogmatic prejudice. In this regard the women are no worse than men, but it is the women who seem to have had the most distressing effect upon Stanley's attempts to deal with his son's madness. This has nothing to do with their endemic female characteristics, but they happen to be the people upon whom Stanley relies the most. Never before the above quoted outburst had Stanley stated or inferred that this was his view of women. The passage is an assembly of the misogynistic opinions, sometimes with verbatim quotes, of Nash, Bert, Cliff, and, ironically, Nowell. Stanley does not believe what he is saying, but throughout the novel he has discovered that there is little point in believing in anything; so, being in a state of despair and confusion and drink, he might as well join in with the men. *Stanley and the Women* does not promote or attempt to excuse misogyny. It is about a man whose world collapses, partly because of what happens to his son and partly because of his own relationships with women. At the beginning of the novel he describes Susan as if he has never met her. 'She looked clever, nervous, humorous, something like devoted or loyal when she gave a person her full attention, and gullible and beautiful'. He is a first-person narrator; he knows his own story and its effects upon him before he tells it, and at this point he knows that his relationship with Susan involves a combination of his own expectations, romantic illusions and failure to properly understand her.

Reviewers like Carey, and Amis's US publishers, might have been better disposed towards the novel if Stanley's outburst had occurred at the beginning, if he had been a little more straightforward in explaining and confessing his own emotional nadir. But Amis is not that kind of writer. His characters are never substitutes for ideas nor even for fully comprehensible states of mind. He engages the reader in complex contemporary issues but he will never allow our interpretive faculties to come to rest upon easy or fashionably decent solutions. Stanley is not Amis, but, in his creation of Stanley, Amis knew that he would provoke hostile responses, particularly amongst those who would carry into their reading of the novel Millett's expectations that male authors must be tolerated for their prejudiced limitations.

Stanley and the Women re-explores themes that had been more explicitly dealt with in *Jake's Thing*. Jake's loss of desire for sex is accurately explained at the end of the novel by his wife, Brenda.

> 'Take away love or sex and the impression ought to be clearer, not distorted by emotions and wishful thinking and so on. But it's the other way round. You used to see as most men see, now you don't. Or it's more like ... What's that stuff they put in ships to keep them from going all over the place?'
> 'What? Oh ... ballast?'
> 'That's right. People's sex drives are like ballast, they keep them steady. It sounds wrong but they do.'

This is indeed a shrewd analysis of Jake's condition. He does not like or dislike women any more than he did before his 'thing', but they have now become strangely alien figures. Previously, whether or not he found a woman sexually attractive did not prejudice his relationship with her as another human being, but it was a necessary element of this relationship. Now, the fact that this carnal response no longer exists unsettles his relationship not only with women but with life, including his own. For Jake substitute Kingsley Amis, novelist, because Brenda's analysis tells us a lot about the function of gender in Amis's fiction.

With the exception of Jenny Bunn, whom I will consider later, Amis's narrative presence is predominantly male. His first-person narrators, John Lewis, Maurice Allington, Douglas Yandell and Stanley Duke, rarely exist for more than 500 words without some reference to women: lack of them, irritation with them, desire for particular representatives of their gender. In the third-person narratives sex is as crucial to the fabric of the text as it was in Jake's previous life. In *Lucky Jim* it is clear, but never explicitly stated by Jim or his narrator, that Christine is the catalyst that projects Jim's inner feelings of dissatisfaction into his eventual act of rebellion. John Lewis's apparent engage-

ments with politics, Welshness, art and professional advancement are never simply that: the uncertainty of *That Uncertain
Feeling* relates to his inability to disentangle his general sense of
unease from his desire for sex. Roger Micheldene, the *One Fat
Englishman*, hates America and Americans but can't quite make
up his mind whether his desire for the American Helene Bang is
the cause or the confirmation of his prejudices. Ronnie Appleyard
of *I Want It Now* regards the fashionable politics of the mid 1960s
with cynical contempt, but he becomes involved with them
because of his love for the archetypal 'subversive' Simona Quick.
Even in the ageist novels, *Ending Up* and *The Old Devils*, sex, be
this a memory or sustained enthusiasm, is an index not just of
character, but of the energy that a character injects into the
narrative. Alun Weaver is the classic case. He is Jake before his
thing: his literary ambitions are a function of his sex drive, and its
continuance, or a remembrance of its consequences, attends his
explosive effect upon all of the other characters.

Male novelists will inevitably impart to their narratives
elements of their perceptions and experience as men, and in
general novels about human life will more frequently than not
engage with human sexuality. But with Amis male sexuality is
not just a routine, contingent feature of the text; it is an ever-
present motivating force.

Amis made a number of attempts to dislodge the male,
heterosexual perspective from the centre of his novels.
Difficulties with Girls (1988) was an update of *Take a Girl Like
You* (1960), but it borrowed its title from an abandoned novel,
planned and partly drafted in the late 1970s and early 1980s, in
which the first-person narrator was to be homosexual. Amis has
always treated homosexuality with a degree of openness and
objectivity. He has never used it as a socio-political hobby-horse,
never assumed a position of self-conscious, and condescending,
liberalism, and never associated this sexual orientation with a
predictable kind of social, intellectual or emotional state.
Colonel Manton's mandarin superiority (*The Riverside Villas
Murder*, 1973) and Bernard Bastable's limitless capacity for hate
(*Ending Up*, 1974) have nothing to do with the fact that they are
homosexuals. But with Captain Max Hunter of *The Anti-Death
League* (1966) Amis began to explore the relationship between
male heterosexuality and homosexuality. He did so by discard-

61

ing the psycho-sexual baggage carried by many previous investigations of the 'condition', and presented Hunter in much the same way as he had presented his heterosexual males. Hunter is a mirror image of Maurice Allington of *The Green Man*. Both are caught in a tension between promiscuity and an equal desire to pursue an emotional commitment to a particular partner. These instincts are irreconcilable, but in Hunter's case they are complicated by the fact that both states are illegal. He can lead a secret life of brief sexual encounters but any form of long-term commitment is an unreal hypothesis. Hunter's friend, James Churchill, comments on his situation:

> 'That's good though, isn't it, according to you? It ought to have taken care of preventing you getting emotionally involved.'
> 'Yes, indeed it ought, but it didn't work like that. I was still feeling my way in those days. I'm in no such danger now.'

Hunter confesses that as a young man he had felt the need for emotional involvement, but not now. In fact he is lying. The reader knows that his alcoholism and his desire to upset the smooth running of Operation Apollo are rooted in his knowledge that he can never satisfy his need for emotional involvement.

There is a tragic irony in Hunter's exchange with Churchill. Churchill's comment carries a slight degree of heterosexual envy: what would it be like to be forever excused even the possibility of an enduring, monogamous relationship? And this hypothesis, fantasy even, is at some point contemplated by practically all of Amis's heterosexual characters. Hunter enacts the fantasy as a living nightmare.

We will never know why Amis abandoned the original *Difficulties with Girls*, but I will offer a hypothesis. Its first-person narrator would have enabled Amis to fully explore the kind of existence that he had briefly examined in the creation of Hunter: the unfinished novel, like *The Anti-Death League*, was to be set in the early 1960s before Roy Jenkins's Act of Parliament legalized homosexuality. All of the conflicting desires and conditions that attend Amis's heterosexual characters – sexuality, lust, commitment, involvement, promiscuity – would be experienced and perceived in a different way. But the novel would have given a horrific twist to this intriguing experiment. The narrator was to be accused by a woman whose advances he has rejected of interfering with her female children. Her husband, his closest friend, knows he is innocent but does not want to lose his mildly psychotic wife by exposing her fabrications in court. I would argue that, while Amis did not present this nightmare of exclusion, victimization, betrayal and secrecy in a single text, he explored different strands of it in a number of novels of the seventies and eighties.

In *The Alteration* (1976) Hubert is offered visions of human sexuality which he understands but, being prepubescent, does not fully comprehend. In chapter 3 his mother and Father Lyall, with whom she is having an affair, try to explain the relationship between human love, involving sex, and love for God. Hubert's brother comments that they 'might as easily explain the colour red to a blind man'. In chapter 4 Ned, the stable boy, responds to his question, 'What happens when you fuck?'

> 'Here it is, now. I grapples her and I near kiss her bloody mouth off the face of her and I gropes the cunt of her till her's all stewed and ready, see? Then I haves the clouts of her and lays the fusby on her back and I shove my pen all the way up her fanny artful and I bang and bang, see?' For a moment longer, he appeared to Hubert angrier than ever, the corners of his mouth drawn tightly back as he puffed out the words. 'I goes on at her cruel till my knob starts to whack her tripes and her cry me mercy, see? Then I feel a start to ... Christ I could ...'

Throughout *The Alteration* the reader encounters a surreal refocusing of very familiar incidents, beliefs and locutions which, for Hubert, cannot be counterpointed against their usual, more stable, context. Hubert's experience of sex involves a choice between abstract theology and self-obsessed violence. Like Hunter and the putative narrator of the abandoned novel, Hubert is the vehicle for a reshuffling of Amis's standard sexual firmament.

The experiment continued in *Jake's Thing* where, as his wife Brenda comments, Jake's life is made unsteady by the removal of its 'ballast', its sex drive. In effect Amis rearranges the already unsettling hall of mirrors that attends the reader's view of Hubert's world. While Hubert is shown the components of adult existence before experiencing the assembled unit, Jake is obliged to relive this existence with its vital element removed.

The borderline between the darkly comic and the horrific is easily crossed, and for Jake in chapter 8 it frequently disappears.

Jake undergoes an 'experimental session' at the hands of a psycho-sexual specialist, Professor Rowena Trefusis, assisted by Jake's regular psychiatrist Dr Rosenburg, the appropriately named Miss Newman and a Ghanaian whose function is not explained. The event is witnessed by eight medical students. Jake is seated on a straight-backed chair, formally dressed in grey suit jacket, regimental tie, grey socks and polished black shoes, but without his trousers and underpants. This mildly surreal juxtaposition of public and intimate presentation is echoed throughout the episode.

Jake is asked to read passages from the flattest and most abstract philosophical tracts, alternated with photographs of naked women undergoing a variety of bizarre and physically strenuous sexual acts. One assumes that this polarity of extreme sexual and non-sexual registers is administered as a means of returning Jake to the position, somewhere between the two, that he had occupied before his 'thing'. But its purpose is continuously parodied and undermined by the manner in which Jake and his specialists are obliged to communicate with each other. Professor Trefusis opens the session by running through their respective curriculum vitae: Jake is 60, married, employed by Oxford University, has a house in Orris Park; she is 36, married to a photographer, has two teenage children and a house up the road in Tooting. This exercise is presumably designed to disperse the prevailing atmosphere of clinical formality. Instead, it becomes a double echo of a lonely hearts column and the kind of modestly suggestive exchange between a male and female at a dinner party. With grim and unintended irony Professor Trefusis moves on without comment to an explanation of how Jake's sexual responses will be measured, via an instrument attached to his penis, on an impressively elaborate set of dials.

All through the session Trefusis and Newman ask Jake polite questions about his sexual responses to the material, whether he is concentrating properly, and the state of his erection. Again, these exchanges carry twisted but very recognizable parallels with a conversation between sexual partners, in bed.

The crescendo of this bizarre double parody of a real and a clinically engineered sexual encounter occurs when Professor Trefusis offers to conclude the session with an instrument called

64

the 'artificial stimulator'. Their exchange shifts brilliantly between an implied memory of Jake's previous experience of intimate contact and the standardized and innocently ambiguous mannerisms of an air stewardess.

> Professor Trefusis came and muttered in his ear, 'Would you like a climax? We can give you one, not out here of course, or we can arrange for you to give yourself one in private.'
> 'I don't think I will, thanks very much all the same.'
> When they parted a few minutes later she said to him, 'I hope to see you again soon.'
> 'Again? Soon?'
> 'After the successful completion of Dr Rosenburg's treatment.'

Chapter 8 tells us a lot about Amis's overall intention in the writing of *Jake's Thing*. Jake does not, via the narrator, reflect upon the significance of the episode. The reader, if he or she is so inclined, is left to assemble an exercise in black comedy from the components of a largely objective report. In the majority of Amis's other third-person novels there is a co-operative alliance between the heterosexual character and the narrator. Sexuality, predominantly male sexuality, is always there, and the text will provide routes between this instinct and practically all other idioms and experiences. Jake's own condition, in which sex is something simultaneously remembered and absent, insinuates itself into the structure of the novel. If any of Amis's other male characters had been substituted for Jake the parallels between the experimental session and the real world of mild flirtation, suggestive discourse and sexual intimacy would have become a running joke shared, implicitly, by character, narrator and reader. Jake's loss of sexual desire detaches him from four decades of familiar emotional, intellectual and verbal operations, and it has a concomitant effect upon the relationship between character, narrator and reader that in Amis's novels had lasted almost as long as Jake's sexual career.

The final traces of the unfinished novel are to be found in *Stanley and the Women* (1984). Stanley, like his unrealized homosexual counterpart, offers a first-person account of someone who no longer hopes to understand the relationship between his sexual instinct and the continuum of love, affection, attachment, betrayal and unfocused nastiness that makes up the rest of his experience of the world. And, like Jake, he breaks the circuit of communication between character and reader: we are offered a version of what he says, does and thinks, but he could be talking to himself.

The question remains as to why, particularly in the late 1970s and early 1980s, Amis continually reshuffled his standard representations of maleness and sexuality? An obvious answer is provided in Jacobs's biography. At the end of the 1970s his marriage with Elizabeth Jane Howard began to break up, and, around the same time, Amis, like Jake, lost his sex drive. If we assume that there was a causal relationship between a sexually active Amis and the confidently arch, humorous and male relationship between text and reader of the fifties and sixties fiction, then we might also assume that Amis's own version of Jake's condition caused him to create a perspective on a world in which sex was ever-present but from which he as a man and a narrator had become detached.

Such creative-biographical speculations are intriguing but must remain inconclusive. After Stanley, the central, heterosexual characters of his novels return to the imperfect but largely predictable confluence of sexuality and everything else that had underpinned his earlier fiction. As I shall show in the last chapter, Amis's experiences of the 1970s had a more enduring effect upon his poetry: it changed for good. Jacobs implies that Amis never regained his sex drive. Does this means that his fictional retrenchment was a remembrance of things past and that the lyrical honesty of his poetry recorded the actuality of things present?

We can never be sure. What we do know is that he did finish a novel called *Difficulties with Girls*. Like its unfinished counterpart it offers a new perspective on male sexuality, but instead of a homosexual narrator it re-engages with an experiment begun in *Take a Girl Like You* (1960). This involved Amis's most prominent woman character, Jenny Bunn. It is a third-person novel but the relationship between character and narrator involves two texts, one occupied by Jenny, the other by Patrick Standish. *Difficulties with Girls* returns us to Jenny and Patrick seven years later, but, in Amis's experience, offers us nearly three decades of retrospection. I would argue that Jenny, 1960 and 1988, provides us with a far more accurate index to Amis's treatment of men, women and sexuality than the reshufflings of maleness in Max Hunter, Hubert, Jake and Stanley Duke.

In *Take a Girl Like You* Patrick maintains the alliance between character and narrator that was established with Jim Dixon: his witty, sardonic, persuasive manner permeates his half of the narrative. Jenny too commands the axis between what she says and does and what she thinks, but she is not the same kind of person as Patrick and nor does she resemble anyone who features as a principal character in any of Amis's other fiction. The following is her response to a poster in the room of her arty and self-consciously French acquaintance, Anna.

> On it was a picture of a man on a blinkered horse pushing a lance into a bull's neck. There was lettering that said GRAN CORRIDA DE TOROS Y MAGNIFICAS NOVEL LADAS, and a lady down in one corner with a man and a fan and a mantilla. She looked a very jolly lady, but foreign. Well, there was nothing wrong with that (though the bull part was horrid); foreigners were colourful and good luck to them. (ch. 7)

The reaction of Patrick or of any of Amis's previous male figures would have been to reflect upon the poster as a rather pretentious and absurd attempt to situate the provocative otherness of European culture in suburban England. But Jenny is conspicuously detached from the habits and mannerisms of these characters. Amis claims to have created her 'as a camera ... to convey a kind of perspective that somebody inside that world couldn't do'.[2] 'That world' is not just the middle-class Home Counties where the novel is set. It is the world of Amis's fiction. The novel is about sex and hypocrisy, and there had been a number of victims of this combination in the earlier novels. Amis creates Jenny as Northern, working-class, sincere, and unashamedly naïve because he needs to have a victim who is also a reliable witness.

In chapter 2 she reflects upon the character of one of her pupils, Michael. He is precocious, a jester and prone to using his verbal skills against his less talented and confident peers.

> Jenny thought what a handsome little boy he was as he reeled along in front of her now, his neat dark fully moulded face permanently over his shoulder to give out his speeches or quizzes. It was hard not to be charmed by his looks and his smile, by his clear pronunciation or by the way that when he thought of it he asked to carry her books for her, like a schoolchild in a story, but nicer...He would be a terrible one for the women when he grew up, Jenny thought, being

not only lively and able to show he knew he was wicked, but also simply incapable of noticing opposition. There seemed to be nothing to be done about it. (ch. 2)

Michael is of course an early version of Patrick, but the narrator implies that Jenny does not consider this parallel worthy of further comment or consideration. She knows Patrick well enough, and her thoughts on there being 'nothing to be done' about the 'terrible one' suggest that she is fully aware of what Patrick will do to her.

In chapter 13 Patrick offers her an informed and sardonic account of her outdated morals. The man she wants, and fantasizes about 'died in 1914 or thereabouts. He isn't ever going to turn up, Jenny, that bloke with the manners and the respect and the honour and the bunches of flowers *and* the attraction...'. Jenny tells him to shut up and that he reminds her of 'someone I used to know, except he never had the gift of the gab like you've got'. The someone is Michael. Her use of the past tense indicates her impossible wish to have known Patrick when he might have been like Michael, when she could have been 'charmed by his looks and smile', but not have encountered the terrible adult he would become. But she does, and when he finally succeeds in having sex with her, when they are both drunk, it is rape.

> She wanted him to stop, but her movements were all the wrong ones for that and he was kissing her too much for her to try to tell him. She thought he would stop anyway as soon as he realized how much off on his own he was. But he did not, and did not stop, so she put her arms round him and tried to be with him only there was no way of doing it and nothing to feel. (ch. 26)

Amis must be commended for his creation of Jenny. She exposes the sexist, élitist, patriarchal confidence of his fiction just as effectively as Millett would have done ten years later.

The novel unsettles the reader's interpretive balance in a number of ways. Patrick is Amis's fictional archetype. Like his predecessors he invites us to sideline our judgement of him as a person because of his wonderfully entertaining presence as a literary character. His acts of betrayal, subterfuge, egotistic retrenchment and adolescent malice would be disagreeable if we actually encountered them, but the amusing interchanges

68

between his inner and outer worlds remind us that he is not real. Jenny disrupts this process. She is so different from Patrick, both as a person and a literary presence, that it is as though the reader is being shown what Patrick would be like without his fictional security. Her flat, styleless description of the rape creates, particularly for a male reader, a sense of unease. Up to that point the difference between their stylistic and intellectual presences might have caused amusement: an exercise in conflict between different classes, levels of sophistication and, yes, between popular images of typically male and female character-istics. Suddenly the fictive game ends. The male reader is invited to feel a degree of shame: the stylistic skills that had protected Patrick from the reader's rebukes are now irrelevant and Jenny's previously amusing transparency discloses a sordid and painful actuality.

Jenny returns home, hung-over and deflowered, and waiting for her are Miss Sinclair, the headmistress of her school, and the mother of John Whittaker, one of her pupils. John and Michael had been playing in an old cottage and John had fallen and broken his ankle. Michael had left him, promising to return with help, but, with symbolic inevitability, he had not. The parallels between Michael and Patrick return, but Jenny does not bother to consider them. What concerns her is Miss Sinclair's decoding of her condition, 'looking her up and down from thatchy hair to muddy shoes, with wine splashed dress playing an important part in between'. She had originally come to see if Jenny would like to visit John, which she offers to do. '"There's no need to put yourself out, Miss Bunn. I'm sure you must have lots of things to do." She gave Jenny the up-and-down treatment in shortened form, then finished: "Goodbye..."'.

Miss Sinclair, as Jenny knows, is saying goodbye to the woman who once was optimistic enough to imagine that Patrick might be different. She returns to Patrick, aware that she will always know that he only means part of what he says and that he will never really know her. 'She would never be able to explain to him what it meant to her not to have gone to John Whittaker when he needed her... She knew more or less what the future would be like and how different it would be from what she had hoped... she must learn to take the rough with the smooth like everybody else'.

Jenny and Patrick return in *Difficulties with Girls* and her prediction is correct. It is 1967 and they are married and living in London. Patrick is an adulterer, and he maintains his other double-life which shows the reader his inner world and, for everyone else including Jenny, filters it through various modes of cynicism and ungenerous wit. Jenny too is largely unchanged, except in her function as a literary device. In chapter 5 she leaves the library with novels by Elizabeth Taylor, Daphne du Maurier and Pearl S. Buck and reflects on her experience with fiction by men.

> They never seemed to give you a feeling of what it was like to be a person, to be inside yourself and experience things happening; they just went about noticing things all the time. And the way they wrote about women, though admittedly that was only half the picture, tended to make them out to be either maddening or funny. (ch. 5)

Jenny seems to have one eye on the novels of Kingsley Amis, apart from the ones she is in.

Amis has one eye on the readers who condemned the misogyny of Stanley and Jake, but Jenny's literary interests become more than an authorial joke. In chapter 16 she finally tells Patrick what she has always thought about him. She does so in the most shrewd and effective way by stating that he has lived as if he were a literary character. She moves to the bookshelves and begins with Amis's old enemy Somerset Maugham. She must have in mind Patrick's ultimatum in their earlier novel: 'I love you and I want to sleep with you. I can't go on seeing you and not' (*Take a Girl Like You*, ch. 22). She does not mention this, but she offers him Maugham as the literary archetype that this ultimatum rejects. 'All about people not doing things that they very much wanted to do because they had an obligation to someone else ... Love without going to bed. What an idea'. Next she opens a copy of Fielding's *Tom Jones*, Amis's and Patrick's favourite. She goes through the novel, emphasizing passages that Patrick has underlined, on how Tom is good-looking, how his rascal temperament makes him nobody's enemy but his own, but how he is open and, with women, inclined to gallantry, and, if they are the women he likes, disposed to 'an obliging complacent behaviour'.

> 'Uncanny isn't it? Really gets you to a T. I particularly like gallantry. I bet you imagined old Henry Fielding winking when he said that. But

now for the clincher. It looks as though you've underlined it heavier than the others, but there's probably nothing in that.
'Though he did not always act rightly, yet he never did otherwise without feeling and suffering for it.'
'So that's alright, isn't it Patrick?' (ch. 16)

She explains that the game must stop, that if she went on behaving as if he were a character in a novel she might, as she has, get on with him but she would abandon her attempts to love him. He asks, 'Is there any hope for us?' and she answers, 'Not as we are. Not unless something happens. And I don't see anything happening.' But at the end something does happen. She becomes pregnant. This is the novel's conclusion.

'How wonderful,' he said ... 'You've done it. Changed everything. You've saved us.'
Jenny was happy. She was going to have him all to herself for at least three years, probably more like five, and a part of him forever, and now she could put it all out of her mind.

The 'him' she refers to is not Patrick, but Patrick's son, a version of Michael but one that she could prevent from becoming a version of Patrick.

The effect created by the closing chapters of the novel brings to mind the postmodern devices of magic realism. Our focus shifts incessantly between suspended disbelief and fictional self-reference. Jenny interprets the real Patrick in the way that a critic, who knows Amis's tastes and affiliations, would interpret his fictional counterpart. At the same time the fiction–reality interplay is part of the fiction. The child is as unreal to us as are Patrick and Jenny, but for her he will be a very real anchor against the fictional world that her husband obliges her to tolerate in her life with him.

Amis's creation of Jenny is a creative counterpart to Millett's interpretive thesis. With his male characters he relies upon the comfortable security of an interplay between them and himself, their creator. Jenny is someone he knows well enough but he does not patronize her by recreating a female version of his male characters and narrators. Instead, she interrupts the easy exchange between male author and male character and she destabilizes it, unsettles it, shows its prejudices and affiliations just as if Amis had stopped the narrative and asked one of his woman readers to walk into it.

71

4

Opinions: Politics, Nation, God, Class and Race

Searching for political opinions in the life and work of Amis is like chasing ghosts. There are suggestions, rumours, apparent facts, but the more we attempt to verify and substantiate them the more diffuse they become. We know that he flirted with communism at school and during his first year at Oxford. He was a supporter and occasional member of the Labour Party during the late forties and fifties. In 1957 he published a leftish pamphlet on *Socialism and the Intellectuals*; by 1967 he had changed his mind about the attractions of Labour and published another on 'Why Lucky Jim turned Right'; and in *An Arts Policy?* (1979) he committed himself to the cultural policies of the new Thatcher government. Read these and you will find that Amis has not really changed at all. His views on the touchstones of post-war political conflict – nationalization, the welfare state, the cold war – are unfixed and contingent. His real reasons for changing sides had nothing to do with the specifics of the British economy or Britain's position in international politics: in terms of its *realpolitik* the Labour Party of the late sixties and early seventies was in any case largely indistinguishable from the Conservatives. Amis's distaste for left-wing politics was fuelled by his perception of socialism as an overarching solution to the question of how life might be made better for everyone. Throughout his life he remained committed to elements of Labour policy that corresponded with his specific personal beliefs – he detested racism and capital punishment particularly – but he disliked anything that resembled a formula, anything which claimed to explain or diagnose the human condition.

In his novels this fickle and detached political stance manifested itself in a number of ways. *Lucky Jim* became associated with a variety of cultural and political trends of the 1950s, although the Angry Young Men and the Movement were anything but united as ideological groupings. The poetry of the Movement was traditional in its style and often regional in its frame of reference, but it carried no attendant political resonances – unless one interprets anti-modernism as a right-wing stance. The Angry Young Men was an umbrella term covering everything from Colin Wilson's very continental exploration of angst in *The Outsider* (1956), through John Osborne's savage exposure of middle-class hopelessness in *Look Back in Anger* (1956) to the presentation of working-class dissatisfaction by the likes of John Braine, David Storey and Alan Sillitoe. Jim Dixon fits into none of these categories. His background is largely unexplored. Ian Carmichael's version of Jim in the Boulting Brothers' film of the book gives him a Northern accent but in the novel Jim remains resolutely non-regional and classless. He despises and ridicules all uses of language as indicators of cultural and intellectual provenance. Indeed, the people he loathes, particularly Margaret and Bertrand, are more closely related to fashionable leftish modes of belief and affiliation than Jim would ever be. If one were to extrapolate a political message from his behaviour he would seem to anticipate the kind of opportunist philistinism that we associate with the Thatcher years of the 1980s. But to do this would be to turn the book into something that it is not. The conclusion of *Lucky Jim* has a certain predictability. Jim has to depart from provincial academic life just as someone who has ridiculed each of the guests at a dinner party, except the one he fancies, would be obliged to leave it as soon as possible. He does not support, rebuke or personify any particular brand of belief or ideology; he dislikes the sham hypocrisy that prompts people to promote them, and for all we know he might come to detest his new boss, the industrialist Gore Urquhart, for the same reason.

John Lewis of *That Uncertain Feeling* is a socialist, but he demonstrates, both consciously and unwittingly, that his commitment is partly hypocritical and partly irrelevant to the things that trouble him, specifically his marriage and his ambitions. He has an affair with Elizabeth Gruffyd-Williams, whose husband Vernon is a local industrialist and council member and who will have a decisive influence upon who is promoted to a modestly senior post in Lewis's place of work, Aberdarcy public library. Lewis's first-person narrative implies as much as it candidly discloses. He detests the social and cultural world inhabited by the Gruffyd-Williamses. He regards their admiration for the Dylan Thomas-like play *The Martyr* as evidence of the middle-class colonization of the real Wales. In his view they enjoy the play's impenetrable style and its pretentious mythological allusions because these are so distant from the way that ordinary, contemporary people speak and live, people they would rather not associate with. The reader knows that this is the way Lewis feels and that his connection with the Gruffyd-Williamses is an act of betrayal, but he is not quite so honest about how he actually deals with the situation. In the middle of their affair he calls Elizabeth from a phone box.

'Hallo', I said. 'Mr Lewis. This is just to tell you that I hate your guts. And your husband's guts. Tell him he can work his Sub-Librarian's job up him. And I hate your friends' guts too. Tell them that librarian fellow of yours says so. And as for you, you stupid bitch...'. 'Hallo,' Elizabeth said in a puzzled tone. 'Hallo, who's that? I can't hear you. Speak up can't you?' I spoke up all right, even screamed at her a little. Then I suddenly noticed that I hadn't pressed button A, and so although I could hear her she couldn't hear me. (ch. 12)

The concluding sentence is double-edged. In his view Elizabeth is indifferent to the real John Lewis. She uses him as a sexual adventure; a handsome, intelligent, but definitely working-class man who can be bought, even constructed, by her husband's feudal influence. But there is a similar game of self-deception taking place in Lewis's offering of his real identity to the reader. At the end of the episode he states that 'Elizabeth had rung off some time ago...I silently thanked the unknown provider of this symbolical reward. Well, no, not symbolical; it was real wasn't it?' Is he asking the reader if the phone call has a degree of fatalistic significance, or is he half-conceding that he knew that she could not hear him. He might have wanted to tell her this, but did he really attempt to do so?

With the possible exception of the phone call, Lewis does not tell lies, but he is by far Amis's most unreliable narrator. He shapes his narrative around his thoughts and frustrations in such a way that we begin to suspect that he is offering us the facts as he wants to see them. The farcical episode in which he 'escapes' from the Gruffyd-Williams's house clothed in the traditional Welshwoman's dress stolen from Elizabeth's theatrical wardrobe is irrational and, he admits, unnecessary. But he does not tell us why he dresses up, particularly in this way, when he would have drawn less attention to himself by sneaking out of the house and travelling home in his own clothes. The costume, for him, probably represents another element of middle-class Aberdarcy's patronizing and sentimentally inaccurate notion of Welshness. He might have wanted to tell them something about this, but instead he stages a satirical play, with himself at its centre. They don't witness it but he does, and so does the reader.

In between chapters 17 and 18 Lewis manages to reassemble his wrecked marriage and move himself and his family to the mining village where he was born, his librarianship exchanged for an office job at the local pit. In chapter 18 Lewis's prose is bathed in a glow of transparent satisfaction: no longer does he need to make events ambiguous, to half-explain them in terms of his principles and his blatant inability to live by them. It is as though he has walked into the stereotypical vision of South Wales mining communities of Richard Llewellyn's *How Green Was My Valley* (1939).

> I took Jean's arm and we moved across the square. The shift at the pit had just emerged and colliers in their neat suits and caps were walking past us or towards the pub. I waved to an overman I knew. An ancient bus half full of more colliers chuntered by. At the pub door we had to wait for a moment until the way cleared ahead of us. To anyone watching it might have looked as if Jean and I, too, were coming off shift.

This is the closing paragraph of the novel and Amis leaves us with a number of questions about Lewis. Is his version of Welsh working-class life any more realistic than the Aberdarcy middle-class's vision of Welsh culture? Does he wrap himself in an ideal of left-wing solidarity as an escape route from his thinly disguised desires and ambitions?

Lewis's dilemmas are echoed in Amis's review of Richard Hoggart's study of working-class life and culture, *The Uses of Literacy*, two years after the publication of the novel. Amis concedes that the social and cultural fabric of South Wales had before the war provided a kind of familial solidarity (though,

75

like Lewis, he reserves a degree of angry contempt for the nonconformist attitude to drink and cinema on Sundays). But he does not regret that all of this is being gradually unweaved by post-war trends such as the welfare state and nationalization: 'if a structure is propped up by unemployment, bad housing and an agonizing fear of debt, then we must kick the prop away'.[1]

This might sound like socialism, but it is pragmatic not ideological socialism. Lewis's socialism is a façade; he substitutes political ideals and a mythological image of working-class culture for a confrontation with reality. Amis's view that socialism distorts the complexities of society and the individual is stated in a letter he wrote to the *Daily Worker* in February 1957. 'I have utterly rejected [Marxism]. No world view, it seems to me, comes within light years of being adequate to the world it professes to categorise. Each fact, each entity, each event is unique. To pretend otherwise is mere Victorian system building. Marxism, I think, does just that. It repels me also by offering certainty instead of truth'. The final sentence might well have been written with Lewis's retreat into the certainties of working-class culture in mind. Amis's Fabian Society pamphlet *Socialism and the Intellectuals* (1957) contains some propositions that could have found a home in the mission statements of Thatcherism. 'I think the best and most trustworthy political motive is self interest', a thesis that Lewis practised with a degree of self-deception. 'I share a widespread suspicion of the professional espouser of causes, the do-gooder, the archetypal social worker who knows better than I do what is good for me'.

Despite his unease with an all-embracing system of socialism, Amis maintains an interest in class that we would associate with a rightish Labour sympathizer. Lewis is implicitly rebuked for his class-consciousness and Roger Micheldene is in some respects his distorted mirror image. Micheldene uses his full nomenclature of Roger H. St John W. Micheldene to impress and intimidate his American hosts, and his presentation of himself as the paradigm of upper-middle-class Englishness, the boorish, intolerant chauvinist in the land of the free, comes close to self-parody. Like Lewis, though for very different reasons, Micheldene attempts to perpetuate the idea that the English class system is alive and well and living in the Edwardian era.

Jenny Bunn and Julian Ormerod of *Take a Girl Like You* provide better examples of how people should deal with their backgrounds. Both are potential archetypes; one is Northern working class with the appropriate accent and mannerisms, the other a Home Counties, ex-RAF pilot with an unearned income and a couple of servants. Neither attempts to disguise, exaggerate or exploit their origins and in many ways they are well matched. Julian tells her that he would like her as a mistress with no commitments and no offence taken if she refuses. She does, and a degree of honesty exists between them thereafter which is conspicuously different from the various levels of pretence, deceit, image building and decoding practised by the rest of the largely middle-class cast, particularly Patrick.

The vast majority of Amis's principal figures, along with their narrator counterparts, inhabit the same relatively classless zone as Amis: not working class but not rich enough to enter the middle-class channels of private school and Oxbridge without scholarships. For most of them and for their author the class system exists and should be acknowledged in fiction, but it exists principally as a façade, an instrument that will invoke particular expectations and associations. In this respect Amis differs from the element of the angry generation represented by Stan Barstow, John Braine and Alan Sillitoe, with which he is, incorrectly, sometimes associated. Sillitoe's *Saturday Night and Sunday Morning* (1958), Braine's *Room at the Top* (1957) and Barstow's *A Kind of Loving* (1960) are radical texts in the sense that they deal with the same moral and existential issues as middle-class fiction but centralize them, without apology or explanation, within the Northern working-class worlds of their characters and narrators. Amis stayed outside this territory partly because it was alien to his own experience, but more significantly because, as he showed with Lewis, he was unhappy with narrative foci and situations that could be explained in conventional, sociological terms.

Amis's most subtle examination of the relation between literature and class occurs in his last novel, *The Biographer's Moustache* (1995). Gordon Scott-Thompson, the biographer, is unimpressed by J. R. P. Fane's fiction. He finds it deliberately obscure and unfocused, its author apparently ignorant of or indifferent to the way that ordinary people speak. Scott-Thompson continues with the project, intrigued that such a writer could have achieved a kind of cultish respect, and towards the end of the novel Fane himself considers the incompatibility of biographer and subject.

> 'May I just suggest quickly that what you delicately called my weaknesses as a writer one might be inclined to see instead as evidence of your unsuitability for your task, an unsuitability nothing to do with the powers of your mind in the ordinary sense?'
> 'But everything to do with the irreducible gap between our respective social groupings.'
> 'Yes, Gordon', said Jimmie with great emphasis. 'Yes exactly so.'
> 'When did you decide that that was a fatal weakness?'
> 'Oh, right at the start, as soon as I heard you speak...'

Fane regards proper literature as something that is socially and genetically determined. He knows, without Scott-Thompson telling him, that his biographer will not like his work, in the same way that he knows that this intelligent but lower-middle-class figure can never become attuned to the habits, activities and affiliations of Fane's social network. Fane's novels do not explicitly promote his political views, but there is an implicit connection between their complacent otherness and his self-conscious detachment from what used to be called the common reading public. Amis despises this, but he is equally contemptuous of left-wing assumptions that culture, particularly literature, should be seen as part of a general remedy for self-improvement and social cohesion.

In his pamphlet *An Arts Policy?*, which is a version of a speech he gave at the 1979 Tory conference, he states:

> It's a traditional lefty view, the belief that anybody can enjoy art, in the same way that everybody is creative. In the words of that old idiot and bad artist Eric Gill 'the artist is not a special kind of man; every man is a special kind of artist'. That's only possible if making mud pies counts as art, which admittedly is beginning to happen. Can you imagine a novel, say, that was relevant to everybody in the United Kingdom including the ones with an IQ of 80? But I think that's what these chaps are getting at.[2]

In his assertion that some people are too stupid to appreciate good writing Amis might sound like a version of Fane, but his real target is the notion of literature as a public service, like housing or the NHS, something that must attend to all manner of disabilities and inequalities. He does not promote Fane's notion of literature as the preserve of the cultural élite, but nor does he see why it should substitute its inherent qualities for discourses that will satisfy, as he sees it, the illusion that all readers are intellectually equal.

Amis's literary tastes and practices are the most reliable index to his political ideas and indeed to his views on a variety of social, ethical and intellectual issues. He never uses his own literary writing as a means of promoting his ideas; this practice constitutes one of his definitions of bad literature. Rather, he uses literature to unshackle contemporary life from the abstract systems that some claim can explain it or resolve its dilemmas. Amis has never summarized his literary ideal, but this can be assembled from his opinions on how other writers used literature as a vehicle for particular brands of belief, ideology or diagnosis.

Amis did not question D. H. Lawrence's abilities as a literary craftsman, but he detested what he saw as Lawrence's employment of them as a means to an end. He refused to take part in the 1950s campaign to un-ban *Lady Chatterley's Lover* because he regarded Lawrence's candid exploration of sexuality as bogus, as a vehicle for the promotion of his ideas. In a 1956 review of a collection of Lawrence's critical essays Amis states that 'the dovetailing of criticism with private obsession makes seven eighths of this collection valueless as criticism, however valuable as a holy book for Lawrentians'[3] and we can substitute 'fiction' for 'criticism'. In Amis's fiction sexuality is something that drives, damages and satisfies different people in different ways; it cannot be diagnosed as part of a solution to the general human dilemma. Similarly, on Evelyn Waugh:

> No novel is a statement, and we should try to fight against making inferences about its author's state of mind. Nevertheless I will succumb to the temptation by suggesting that the 25 year old Waugh, rather than go mad or commit suicide, was in real need of something that offered an explanation or an excuse for the horrors of existence. We all know what Waugh found – to his artistic detriment.[4]

Amis's point is that, even if we know nothing of the life of Waugh, an experience of the later novels will show us that their author is not only a Catholic, but is using his considerable

79

literary talent to advertise the benefits of Catholicism to his reader. This, in Amis's view, is an artistic defect because in novels such as *Brideshead Revisited* (1945) the religious transformation of the principal character will not only explain for him the moral complexities of his own life but will have a similar effect upon the reader's experience of the narrative: the novel becomes less a representation of the world and more a representation of a world filtered through the author's confident belief in a system that explains it.

Amis existed half-way between agnosticism and reluctant atheism, and we know this only from biographical evidence. He never allowed his lack of faith or his sceptical view of other peoples' to influence the behaviour of his principal characters or the shape of his narrative. The Revd Ayscue in *The Anti-Death League* has his beliefs challenged, but never quite destroyed, by his experience of what human beings have, by choice and obligation, become. What remains of his faith provides him with a degree of consolation, but it does not offer a solution to the ethical and emotional questions raised by the novel. The Revd Tom Sonnenschein of *The Green Man* transforms Ayscue's personal anxieties into noisy, confident and very fashionable dogma. He is an ultra-liberal clergyman, reluctant to conduct Allington's service of exorcism because he does not believe in an afterlife. 'Immortality's just a passing phase. Basically it was thought up by the Victorians, especially the early Victorians, as a sort of guilt thing. They'd created the evils of the Industrial Revolution, they could sense what kind of ghastly bloody monster capitalism was going to turn out to be, and the only refuge from hell on earth they could think of was a new life away from the smoke and the stink and the cries of the starving kids' (ch. 4). Goaded by Diana, Allington's occasional lover, Sonnenschein eventually asserts that Christianity is now only relevant as a rallying point for the fight against injustice and oppression in Greece, Rhodesia, Mozambique, Ulster, Angola .... God himself in his chat with Allington is unhappy with that 'posturing idiot Sonnenschein making me out to be a suburban Mao Tse-tung', while conceding that the Church is still a significant presence in humanity's struggle with good and evil. God, the character, does not offer a solution to contemporary arguments on whether Christianity, Marxism or a fashionable combination of the two is

80

the best approach to life; and Amis, with typically dark humour, has introduced the ultimate, unchallengeable Authority as a means of destabilizing the notion that the human condition can be neatly explained in terms of all-inclusive systems of belief or political analysis.

The Green Man could have become the kind of neo-gothic novel of ideas in which Iris Murdoch specializes. Instead it shows that the complex intellectual systems that accumulate around the generally secure perspectives of middle-class England are verbose bunkum when the individual has to confront the actuality of evil and malice; in this case Allington's battle with an agent of Satan who almost kills his daughter.

The most reliable parallels between Amis's life and his fiction involve the issues of race and nationality. I Like It Here (1958) earned him a reputation for little-England xenophobia, principally because it is his least fictional novel. Amis admits that he 'did once... try to put real people on paper and produced what is by common consent my worst novel!'[5] The Somerset Maugham Award for Lucky Jim contained the condition that Amis spend several months abroad, which he and his family did, in Portugal; and this provided the material for Garnet Bowen's story. Amis was a new writer. He could have used the visit as a basis for a narrative, a mood, that were not so firmly rooted in British mannerisms, contexts and culture as his first two novels had been. Indeed he toyed with the idea of a mildly experimental hybrid of fact and fiction in which Jim Dixon is sent by his boss, Gore Urquhart, to Portugal where he meets Kingsley Amis. Instead he adopted a two-pronged assault upon the notion of abroad. The first, which created the novel's provincialist reputation, involved a catalogue of superior Ealing Comedy episodes based upon the primitive state of Portuguese bathrooms and transport; all, apparently, true. The second was a little more serious and purely fictional. Bowen is sent to track down the mysterious English author Wulfstan Strether. Strether represents Amis's notion of abroad not as an actual experience – Amis enjoyed most of his travels – but as an artistic gesture that to him seemed to have become a necessary qualification for highbrow literary status. Strether is a modernist whose persona and his quoted writing are designed to bring to mind D. H. Lawrence, Samuel Beckett, James Joyce and a whole retinue of

British-born authors who, while not completely abandoning their language, feel that it can only properly be deployed from somewhere else.

Amis the writer did indeed 'like it' more in Britain than anywhere else, chiefly because the texture of his fiction depended upon a kind of dialogue with his readers. He remained amazed that *Lucky Jim* had been translated, and sold, in fourteen languages. This novel, along with most of his other work, involves a continual interchange between elements of the text that are so familiar that they could be verbatim recordings, and elements which project the writing into self-evident orchestrations and twistings of perceived reality. He needed to be in Britain to keep in touch with the former. His most fantastic fictions, *The Anti-Death League, The Green Man, The Alteration* and *Russian Hide-and-Seek,* work best in their counterposings of the solidly familiar features of England with narratives and conditions that are blatantly fantastic.

But Amis the man and the author was never a nationalist. He liked Britain because there was nothing particularly characteristic about it to like. His political shift to the right was not so much a matter of specific ideological principle, but more a feeling that the leftist elements of the Labour Party seemed to want to turn Britain into a disagreeable version of Eastern Europe; disagreeable because it would be predictable rather than, as he saw it, an engaging mess.

Wales was Amis's alternative to the writer abroad. He spent the formative part of his life as a writer there as a lecturer in Swansea University. *That Uncertain Feeling* (1955) is about politics, class and sex, but it would not be the novel that it is without the uncertain sense of Welshness that pervades practically all of Lewis's acts, thoughts and encounters. He, like Amis, detests the use of national identity as a substitute for an open, general perception of literature and culture. But at the same time working-class Welsh idioms and habits occupy a privileged centre ground in the fabric of his text. This ambivalent, paradoxical interplay between disapproval and enthusiasm is replayed in Amis's 1959 essay 'Where Tawe Flows', an account of the Welsh National Eisteddfod (in *What Became of Jane Austen?*). Amis is mildly annoyed that everything, including his press badge, is in Welsh and English; but he is impressed by the fact that the versifier best deserving of the bardic chair is discussed, at work, by the clerk and the shopkeeper; even more so because they are the judges. England, he implies, has turned the activity of serious writing, particularly poetry, into a token of middle-class intellectualism while Welsh literature, at least in Welsh, is more pervasive, and classless. His perspective is partly romantic, partly pragmatic. His own poetry, like that of his friend Philip Larkin, is clever but accessible: anyone can read it. At the same time one suspects that he perceives the Eisteddfod as an endearing fantasy, that the transcendent clubbishness of writing in Welsh could never be transplanted to the diversities and complexities of an English-speaking readership, in England, Wales or anywhere else.

Amis frequently returned to Wales from his base in London, and his contacts with friends from his Swansea days inspired *The Old Devils* (1986). The shifting perceptions of Wales and Welshness in Lewis's narrative and Amis's essay are cleverly distributed among its main characters, and brilliantly enacted in the relation between Alun Weaver and his narrator. Alun knows that his various books and TV programmes on Wales are shameless distortions of actuality, particularly his exploitation of US and English taste for the poet Brydan, a thinly disguised version of Dylan Thomas. He is mildly uneasy with this, but he never allows his unease to undermine his addiction to money and fame. In chapter 2, after Alun and Rhiannon get off the train from London, the narrator discloses his thoughts regarding the bilingual sign for Taxi/*Tacsi*; 'for the benefit of Welsh people who had never seen the letter X before'. A taxi arrives, 'a London model taxi, rare in this part of the world. Something about this displeased him'. Alun wants a saloon so he can sit next to the driver and have a proper conversation, and he explains this to Rhiannon.

> 'Well, you know, I always like talking to drivers and people when I'm here. Very Welsh thing. It's a completely different relationship to what you get in England. Difficult to explain'.
> 'You needn't to me. I am Welsh too as it happens. Boyo.'
> 'Piss off,' he said...

Rhiannon's satirical 'Boyo' reminds Alun that he is now in Wales, and that he should save his patronizing discourse for his non-Welsh viewers and readers. Alun is an irredeemable hypo-crite, but his briefly sincere anger at the Taxi/*Tacsi* sign is a slender thread which links him to the rest of the cast, who explore in different ways their different allegiances to a place and a nationality. At the opening of the novel Malcolm and Gwen Cellan-Davies discuss Alun's exploitation of the Brydan industry, which includes the shameless imitation of Brydan's style in his own poetry.

> Gwen put her head on one side and gave the little frowning smile she used when she was putting something to someone, often a possible negative view of a third party; 'wouldn't you have to agree that he follows Brydan at, er, an altogether lower level of imagination and craftsmanship?'
> 'I agree that compared with Brydan at his best, he doesn't –'
> 'You know what I mean'.

He does. She means sex. Gwen's introduction of this subtext is shrewd and cruel. Malcolm spends his spare time attempting a translation of a medieval Welsh epic into the kind of English that will connect the Wales of today with its first language and its past. Though never stated, this is his authentic alternative to Alun's exploitation of poetry and bogus Welshness, and his motive is not unrelated to his knowledge that Alun's fraudulent sincerity once got him into bed with Gwen.

The arrival of Alun causes each of the old devils to consider again the various experiences of deceit, failure and expediency that make up their past and contribute to their present. Versions of Wales – bogus, exportable Welshness, shabby post-industrial Welshness, their half remembered–half denied love for the place – slide in and out of their thoughts and arguments about sex, drink, money, literature and everything else, and the brief exchange between Malcolm and Gwen sets the tone for the entire novel. The novel is about Wales in the sense that it brilliantly captures the idioms, habits and lifestyles of its inhabitants, circa 1986; and in his continual intermeshing of this subject with every other emotive condition Amis offers us his own vision of Welshness: the fact that it insinuates itself subtly into the lives of the people who disagree on what it means is far better than a definition.

Politics, national identity and class are subjects that Amis ties closely into the broader fabric of his characters' lives. Often one of these topics will be given special emphasis but will always carry with it perspectives and associations that guarantee a short circuit in the line between the book and the author's opinions. He made only one exception to this method – with racism. Racism had become an element of British life during the waves of emigration from India, Pakistan and the West Indies in the fifties and sixties, but Amis's first recorded encounter with it occurred on his visit to Nashville in 1967. At Vanderbilt University he met Professor Walter Sullivan whose sabbatical had created the space for his visiting post. At dinner Sullivan declared that he never gave 'A grades to Jews or nigras'. It soon became evident to Amis that this statement was not a parody of low-life bigotry, and, even worse, that Sullivan's 'beliefs' were firmly entrenched in the university, even among undergraduates. This experience lies behind Ronnie Appleyard's encounter with Mr Mansfield at a Fort Charles dinner party in *I Want It Now* (1968). Mansfield says:

> '*and*...we've solved the Negro problem. By realizing there is no problem, except keeping 'em down. That's what I said, keeping 'em down. They're inferior, they always will be inferior, and we in the South have the honest-to-God common sense to realize it. There's your so-called Negro problem solved. Simple.... The only way to keep the Negro in his place is by *fear*. The only argument he understands is the *lash*.' (ch. 3)

Ronnie, whose commitment to any 'cause' is dependent upon its benefits to his media image, suddenly becomes dangerously sincere. He ridicules Mansfield as 'barbaric, inhumane, foolish, ignorant, outmoded...' and is ejected from the house by his host Lady Baldock. Lady Baldock's Christian name is Juliette, which by no coincidence echoes that of the intelligent, beautiful Nashville undergraduate Julie Smith who had told Amis, again at a party, that the Northern states 'didn't know how to keep 'em [Nigras] down'. Amis's experience of Southern American racism caused him to suspend his reluctance to channel his beliefs transparently through his fictional character. In his next novel, *Girl 20* (1971), he returned to form.

Gilbert Alexander is Sir Roy Vandervane's chauffeur and general assistant. He is black and his relationship with the narrator Douglas Yandell enables Amis to deal with race in the way that he had used Lewis to deal with class and Wales. They meet first when Gilbert collects Douglas from the station.

'What a nice car,' I said. 'Is it yours?'
'You think a stupid nigger could never make the bread to buy himself a status symbol like this?'
'Well since you mention it, it would be remarkable, certainly.'

Gilbert knows that Douglas knows the car belongs to Vander-vane and he responds with an angry self-parody. The first part of their exchange involves Douglas playing the role of the educated racist and Gilbert probing the depths of this persona.

'Where do you come from?' I asked.
'London.'
'Oh I see.'

Douglas clearly expects the term 'come from' to provoke a more elaborate reaction to its national and ethnic overtones, but Gilbert neutralizes this strategy. They arrive at the gates of the Vandervane house. Gilbert sits motionless, and Douglas asks,

'Would you like me to open those?'
'If you think it won't soil your fine hands.'
'I'll risk it.'

Instead of defusing the tension with an unprovocative 'I'll open the gates', Douglas, with his question, invokes the master-servant subtext.

Gilbert is the first to raise the stakes in their game of self-parodies.

'You are an imperialist racist fascist'.
'But how on earth did you know?'

Gilbert refers to the newspaper for which Douglas works as classical music reviewer, and Douglas asks

'What about it?'
'It's a white supremacist colonialist organisation.'
'Of course, but I'm not an employee of theirs, I just do regular pieces for them. And colonialist music is rather hard to...'.

Douglas's cool sidestep causes Gilbert to stop the game. Both characters abandon their assumed roles and, as if they had just read the passage, consider their reasons for taking them on. Gilbert asks, 'Don't you think it's a bloody serious accusation, to call you a fascist?' No, answers Douglas: fascist, communist, bourgeois are labels. 'I just don't care about any of that'. Gilbert wonders what he does care about, and he tells him: 'me and my interests, chiefly musical'.

There is a delicate, resonant irony in the exchange. Douglas, the narrator, is precise in his account of it because it prefigures his gradual discovery of his own shortcomings. He triumphantly discloses his real persona to Gilbert and he does not show any interest in what lies behind Gilbert's performance. By the end of the novel he realizes that this is the way he conducts his life. Douglas's girlfriend Vivienne abandons him for Gilbert because Douglas, despite being informed and decent, does not care. Penny exchanges Gilbert for Douglas for the same reason. Gilbert knows and cares about her heroin addiction; Douglas is too self-possessed to notice it. The issue of race informs the novel as a dramatic subplot. Douglas plays the game with Gilbert in order to distance himself from, to demystify, the contemporary left-wing fashion for anti-racism: intellectuals like me, he implies, do not notice colour. And Amis shows us gradually, cautiously, that such an attitude is not too far from a failure to notice and care about anything.

Douglas's exchange with Gilbert might well have been in Amis's mind when he wrote chapter 4 of *Jake's Thing* (1978), because in this he provokes the reader in much the same way that his two earlier characters had played games with each other's responses. The chapter involves Jake's first encounter with the psycho-sexual specialist, Proinsias Rosenburg MD, MA (Dip Psych) of 878 Harley Street.

> Jake found himself closeted with a person he took to be a boy of about seventeen, most likely a servant of some kind, in a stooped position doing something with an electric fire. 'I'm looking for Dr Rosenburg' he said.
> It was never to cut the least ice with him that the other did not reply, 'Ah now me tharlun man, de thop a de mornun thoo yiz' – he might fully as well have done by the effect ('Good morning' was what he did say).

The following ten pages are crowded with references to Rosenburg's Irishness. After Rosenburg asks him when he last masturbated, the narrator tells us that 'It took Jake a little while to get the final participle because the Irishman had stressed it on the third syllable'. Rosenburg explains the Germanic origin of his surname and fails to understand Jake's reference to Austria as a more appropriate location. The narrator discloses Jake's unease at 'being asked to believe in a student of the mind who didn't know where Freud had come from'. Jake tests him further with a coat-trailing allusion to 1848 as the year that his own, French, ancestors had arrived in England; and, as he had suspected, Rosenburg seems to be unaware that anything special had happened in Paris in 1848.

Rosenburg's most bizarre characteristic is his habit of switching idioms and frames of reference without warning. He shifts seamlessly from his explanation of his surname to his rate of seventeen pounds fifty a session and from an apparent interest in Jake's profession to the weight of his wife. Worst of all he does this without any awareness of its darkly comic effect. At the end of their session he introduces Jake to the nocturnal mensurator which, he explains, will measure the frequency, duration and size of Jake's night-time erections. He tells him how to fit the plastic loop to his penis, how an erection is registered on the disc and circuit breaker and that he should not forget to turn off *both* switches when he gets out of bed. All this is delivered by someone who, as the narrator reminds us, 'didn't really talk like an O'Casey peasant, his articulation was too precise for that, but he did talk like a real Irishman with a largely unreconstructed accent'.

The creeping sensation of Rosenburg as a figure beyond parody is given a crisp finale when he hands Jake his visiting card.

'Proinsias. Is that a German name?'
'Irish. It's pronounced Francis. The correct Gaelic spelling. I take it you've no objections to exposing your genitals in public.'

The last sentence refers to Jake's forthcoming appointment with Dr Trefusis, but read it with a particular emphasis on 'your' and its potential as the punch line to the running Irish joke becomes apparent. The speech acquires a degree of continuity, with an implied subclause: 'as I do, habitually, being Irish and given to talking bollocks'.

This interpretation is of course my own. Neither Jake nor the narrator comments upon this ideogrammic juxtaposition of proud Irishness and verbal absurdity: the punch line, if there is one, is left to the reader. Indeed, throughout the chapter there is no explicit proposal that Rosenburg's surreal persona is causally related to his nationality. Read it carefully and you will find that Amis uses the relationship with Jake and the narrator in a way that unsettles my initial reading.

The fact that Rosenburg is Irish is registered exclusively by Jake, to the extent that it becomes something of an obsession. It is clear that the O'Casey parody at the beginning, though offered to the reader by the narrator, is Jake's. Jake's references to Austria and 1848 as tests of intellectual depth are by no means objective criteria. It is plausible that Rosenburg decides to ignore the Austria–Freud connection because he is not certain that this is what Jake has in mind; and he would not want to insult or patronize his patient with his own bout of intellectual name dropping. Similarly Rosenburg's failure to pick up the thread of 1848 causes Jake to evaluate him as he does his useless students: but Rosenburg is not facing a multiple choice test in European history; he is interviewing a patient.

At no point in the chapter is it suggested either by Jake or the narrator that Rosenburg is professionally incompetent or that his techniques are in themselves discreditable. Instead we are offered a split perspective. Jake is the focus for the Irish allusions while Rosenburg's rather eccentric verbal mannerisms are documented, objectively, by the narrator. The cheap joke, the one about the Irish psychoanalyst, is suspended between the two perspectives. Jake implies it but he does not, as his fictive predecessor Jim Dixon would have done, make it the basis for an interior exercise in mockery. This is left to the reader, depending of course upon the kind of reader that you happen to be.

Throughout the novel a variety of flagrantly reactionary discourses – anti-women, anti-feminist, anti-youth, mildly racist – gather at the intersection between Jake's narrative focus and the narrator's more objective role. The particular function of this technique is to emphasize the effect of Jake's loss of interest in sex, his 'thing'. His narrative carries a residual memory of what Jake was like before: tolerant, liberal, open-minded, decent and, of course, sexually active. The implied conclusion is that Jake's sexual appetite is the peg that held his endearing characteristics together; but it would be wrong to regard the novel as simply a neo-Freudian diagnosis of maleness. The narrator neither condemns nor collaborates with Jake's temperamental unpleasantness. He opens it up to the reader in a way that invites us into the text, either as people who might, guiltily, identify with Jake's musings or who might respond to them with varying degrees of revulsion. At the end of this experience, we are left with an unanswerable question: is Jake Amis or is Amis showing us Jake?

In a more general sense the technique is typical of Amis's use of social and political allusions, which can only be described as a kind of textual ventriloquism. Attitudes, opinions, mannerisms, fashionable and unfashionable responses will be sewn into the narrative so that the reader does not have to suspend disbelief. Amis knows exactly how to create feelings of anger or sympathy in the reader that are just as real as those which attend our actual conversations or overheard statements. Concurrently he will make certain that when the reader attempts to follow through his/her response, to extrapolate a particular moment to the polemical function of the novel as a whole, or perhaps as an index to Amis's own coherent ideology, the illusion vanishes. What remains, however, is a feeling of disorientation. Amis draws us so cleverly, either as hostile or sympathetic participants, into his fictional world that when he withdraws the invitation we are left with the mildly embarrassing knowledge that we were trying to interpret the novel as we wanted it to be. It never is what we want it to be because Amis never allows his textual fabric to unravel and disclose a particular or reliable set of ideas.

Satire and social commentary have since Fielding been durable features of the English novel. Austen, Thackeray, Dickens, Forster, Waugh, Huxley, Orwell and Lodge have practised very different forms of the comedy of manners. Irrespective of their faith or lack of it in underlying human characteristics, each has drawn upon transient social and political registers, skilfully reproducing them and variously exposing them as fraudulent, selfishly motivated or as substitutes for serious confrontations with the contemporary world. Amis does this too, but more than any of his predecessors or contemporaries he also entraps the reader in the text. The object of Amis's satire is deceptively apparent, but never clearly defined. The more we search for a coherent centre, the more it becomes clear that the satirical object is ourselves. His novels are halls of mirrors: we recognize elements of ourselves, while at the same time we can be angered by the inaccurate distortion of features that we regard as fundamental characteristics of ourselves and our friends. For physical features substitute political, social and ideological ideals. Amis never allowed his fiction to become a vehicle for particular opinions, but what he did was to recreate in the reader the emotive underpinnings of our own opinions. Tom Paulin, for example, read *Jake's Thing* as if Jake was Amis. 'Reading Amis's prose is like getting kicked in the stomach – I found myself retching at its sheer awfulness...It's a sad assertion of defeated machismo, and if anyone thinks that the phrase "all according to him" refers to Jake and not Amis, then they can't tell crude bad artistry from good. [Jake is] a bloody-minded, insular, beer-swilling, xenophobic, philistine with a thick neck and a truculent manner. He hates wogs, he hates the young, and he wishes women would disappear as soon as it's over. Although this choleric figure has been lying low of late, he has dictated a novel to a battered amanuensis called Kingsley Amis'.[6] Amis enjoyed reviews like Paulin's, because Paulin has become part of the text; Jake, for him, is very real. There is an unintended irony in his charge that the reader who perceives Jake as a fictional character 'can't tell crude bad artistry from good' because Amis's artistry has lured Paulin into the fictional world so easily. There is a devious subtlety in the interplay between Jake and his fictional world, and the fact that Paulin's anger has blinded him to it is a sufficient guarantee of its effectiveness.

5

Poetry

Amis began his career as a poet long before he had published any fiction. His first poetry collection, *Bright November*, was published in 1947 by the Fortune Press whose owner, the notorious Reginald Ashley Caton, reappears as L. S. (Lazy Sod) Caton in Amis's first five novels, before being killed off in *The Anti-Death League* (1966). The real Caton was probably worse than his fictional counterpart. He dealt in property and pornography and the ironically titled Fortune Press was partly a tax dodge for his less respectable activities. It did, however, publish a number of respectable writers, including Roy Fuller, Dylan Thomas, C. Day Lewis, Alun Lewis and Amis's friend Philip Larkin who advised Amis to take his first collection to Caton.

Bright November is a stylistic hybrid. Amis is trying to find a poetic voice and he relies frequently upon other people's. His confident, unborrowed persona would not begin to appear until the 1950s. It features most prominently in his 1956 collection *A Case of Samples* and begins to change in *A Look Round the Estate* (1967). The latter was his final original collection. *Collected Poems 1944–1979* appeared in 1979 and after the 1970s his poetic output was infrequent.

'Letter to Elisabeth' is effectively his first published poem. It is addressed to Elisabeth Simpson, a married woman with whom he began a two-year affair in 1942: *Bright November* is dedicated to her. The poem's style carries echoes of T. S. Eliot, W. H. Auden and other poets of the 1930s. The metre and syntax recall passages from Eliot's *Four Quartets*. Like Eliot, Amis maintains a flexible, uneven version of the iambic pentameter, and he exhibits a cautious delicacy in the placing of noun and verb phrases within the structure of each line and across its enjambed relation to the next. At one point Amis slows the pace and contemplates both the meaning and the concrete actuality of the words.

> There shall be no more No nor no more Yes,
> No need for speech or thought. A time for feeling,
> Uniting lovers in the spring...

The internal rhymes and repetitions both suspend and emphasize the sense of the language, and it is more than likely that when writing this Amis turned his eye and ear to the opening of section V of Eliot's 'Burnt Norton'.

> Words after speech, reach
> Into the silence. Only by the form, the pattern,
> Can words or music reach
> The stillness...

For metaphor and figurative frame of reference Amis goes to Auden. The loudest echo comes from Auden's famous 'Lullaby'. Amis's opening lines,

> Even the perfect year must finish, love
> Just as the winter we found hard to leave,

resonate with Auden's,

> Lay your sleeping head my love
> Human on my faithless arm;

Throughout the poem Amis, like Auden, constantly juxtaposes the imagery of the body and sexual contact with universal notions of pain and joy and with the mundane familiarities of waiting in streets and writing notes. The closing lines, like Auden's, echo and revise the figures of the first, particularly in their focus on the relation between the passage of time and the endurance of love. Amis:

> The eyes that looked goodbye will look at love
> As from this sleep we know ourselves alive.

Auden:

> Noons of dryness find you feel
> By the involuntary powers,
> Nights of insult let you pass
> Watched by every human love.

Amis showed an admirable degree of honesty in including

'Letter to Elisabeth' as the first of his *Collected Poems* because it sometimes betrays characteristics that he would later as a critic attack as a tendency 'to make words mean what [the poet] wants them to mean'.

> my scene has shifted, but
> Still flows your northern river like a pulse,
> Carrying blood to bodies at the poles.

If the river is the bloodstream how can it also carry blood 'to' bodies? And are the 'poles' the points of physical separation between him and her, or are they part of the body/landscape metaphor? One suspects that once Amis had decided to employ adventurous tropes and maintain the off-rhyme couplet scheme he found himself compromising clarity for sound. With a peculiar irony the lines echo a similarly disorientating passage from a 1934 poem by a writer whom Amis regarded as vastly overrated, Dylan Thomas:

> Dawn breaks behind the eyes;
> From poles of skill and toe the windy blood
> Slides like a sea;

'Radar' could almost be a parody of Auden with large doses of Lewis's *The Magnetic Mountain* thrown in. 'Belgian Writer' juxtaposes the erotic, the mundane and the surreal in a vision of the otherness of Europe that Auden had already explored in 'The Capital', 'Brussels in Winter' and 'Gare du Midi'.

But there are also in *Bright November* hints of the real Amis. In 'Beowulf' we hear Amis the comic describing the Old English warrior as perhaps rather bored with his modern role as an Oxbridge examination question: 'he lay down to sleep,/Locking for good his massive hoard of words (Discuss and illustrate)'. In 'Bed and Breakfast' the imagery is more self-consciously provincial and non-cosmopolitan than in the Auden borrowings. It takes us to and never leaves the bedroom of a dull boarding house where love or disappointment might have been felt. The second stanza addresses a 'stranger' who will come to the same room to unpack, and who should expect from the speaker

> nothing but a false wish
> That going, you ignore all other partings
> And find no ghosts that growl or whinny of
> Kisses from nowhere, negligible tears.

Is the addressee some putative, equally anonymous visitor to the dull room? Or is this 'stranger' the woman with whom the speaker will share the room and who is warned of the transient, ghostly nature of their encounter? The questions remain unanswered; and the effect of banal ordinariness mingled with potential significance echoes that of early Larkin pieces such as 'Past days of gales' and 'Getaway', and looks forward to characteristic features of the 1950s 'Movement' style. Events, places, objects have in themselves no immanent qualities or resonances; things happen, but their 'meaning' involves a mixture of resolute cynicism and unobtrusive stylistic skill.

Amis never liked to be associated with particular schools of writing, but the post-war trend in British poetry towards anti-modernist realism and anti-Romantic empiricism is a key feature of his 1950s verse. In 'Against Romanticism', published in *A Case of Samples*, Amis describes what happens when a Romantic poet chooses a location for his verse.

> Over all, a grand meaning fills the scene
> And sets the brain raging with prophecy
> Raging to discard real time and place
> Raging to build a better time and place.

Amis would prefer it

> if images were plain,
> Warnings clearly said, shapes put down quite still
> Within the fingers' reach, or else nowhere...

'Against Romanticism' is transitional and self-referential. It looks back to what Amis had been trying to do in 'Bed and Breakfast' and it announces that in *A Case of Samples* time and place will be far more 'real', images 'plain' and things very 'clearly said'.

What it does not say and what makes *A Case of Samples* important is that Amis the poet had become a mirror image of Amis the novelist. His fiction always involves a balancing act between transparency and the subtle foregrounding of devices that make transparency possible. We suspend disbelief, but Amis is always there to show us how he has made this possible. The fifties poems range through a variety of poetic subgenres. Some, recalling 'Bed and Breakfast', are reflections anchored firmly to specific moments or places. Others are narratives, condensed short stories, often involving a persona that is clearly

Amis himself. Some are intellectual puzzles turning inward upon their own language and points of reference. The feature that unites them is their self-evident, self-conscious mastery of style and subject, a sense of Amis standing just outside the poem but always close enough to show us how and why he is writing it.

In 'A Song of Experience' the narrator and his friends encounter a travelling salesman in a pub, and he tells them of the women he has known and seduced. The tone is informal, familiar; the conversational diction is slipped into the quatrains as easily as the traveller slips in, and out, of the lives, emotions and bodies of his women.

> He tried all colours, white and black and coffee;
>> Though quite a few were chary, more were bold;
> Some took it like the Host, some like a toffee;
>> The two or three who wept were soon consoled.

The poem seems to be no more than a smirking celebration of the traveller's Jack-the-laddish lifestyle, but something else is going on. It is not only about the experiences of the traveller; it involves Amis and the reader in an exploration of the relationship between poetry and sex.

> The inaccessible he laid a hand on,
>> The heated he refreshed, the cold he warmed
> What Blake presaged, what Lawrence took a stand on,
>> What Yeats locked up in fable, he performed.

The narrator, definitely Amis, derides the literary tradition which turns the pure pleasure of sex into apocalyptic metaphors. It is as though Amis has set himself a particular task: write a poem about sex that does not either turn it into something greatly symbolic or, like Eliot with the young man carbuncular and the secretary, patronize those who simply enjoy it. He complicates the task by using a form that brings to mind a tradition that he despises. The quatrain, the double rhymes, the trisyllabic ballad metre and the allusive title recall Blake's songs; and they invoke a high cultural habit, practised also by Wordsworth in *Lyrical Ballads*, of using the ballad form as a concession to the low-life idioms of the poem's intriguing specimens. Amis succeeds in his task by maintaining an ironic distinction between the self-consciously poetic medium and a subject that the medium must by its very nature fail to comprehend. The last quatrain is a wonderful example of how to mix a genre with a subject that resists it, and put the genre in its place.

> I saw him, brisk in May, in Juliet's weather,
>   Hitch up the trousers of his long-tailed suit,
> Polish the windscreen with a chamois leather,
>   And stow his case of samples in the boot.

The Shakespearean allusions of the first line are left in the background as the diction and habits of the real world take over. We know that the traveller in the long-tailed suit, polishing his windscreen, would not know or care about Juliet, but Amis, through his sheer stylistic versatility, makes sure that he belongs, unpatronized and unexplained, in the same poem.

In 1985 Tony Harrison published a poem called *V* in which the style and idiom of Gray's 'Elegy in a Country Churchyard' encompass a graffiti-sprayed, skinhead-infested, cemetery in present-day Leeds. It was widely celebrated as a daring act of cultural reinvention, a revival of hidebound tradition with living language. Amis's 'Song of Experience' must surely be acknowledged as its precedent.

'Alternatives' engages with a very different catalogue of effects and expectations. The first three stanzas offer a brief, cinematic narrative. A girl is alone in a dark house playing the piano. A man moves from the pavement and up the stairs. He enters the room and strangles her. In the fourth stanza Amis stops the film and asks if the reader would like to alter the narrative. Perhaps the house should be empty; or maybe she knows and is expecting the man, whose hands will move not to her throat but to her breasts. This could have been a tempting model for the kind of neo-gothic, twist-in-the-tale short story that Amis liked to write. But what makes it more impressive as a poem is the way that Amis alters the narrative focus without changing the style and idiom that contain it. In the first three stanzas the pace of the narrative is governed by the distribution of clinical, visual images across a kind of loose blank verse.

> It starts: a white girl in a dark house
> Alone with the piano, playing a short song;
> Lilies and silk stand quiet, silent the street,
> The oil lamp void of flame.

The verse form measures the language, with the result that

97

when the movements and acts of the murderer are described they maintain the same degree of stillness as the opening passage. The overall effect is of inevitability: the narrative moves, but the verse form seems to capture its entirety like a photograph.

In the fourth stanza the narrator addresses the reader directly, but the formal effect does not change. The alternative narrative is offered, yet it never quite separates itself from the original. The decoded images are different, while in the language of the poem they seem to be part of the same story.

> Or would you rather she smiled as she played,
> Hearing a step she knows, and sitting still,
> Waited for the hands to move, not round
> Her throat, but to her eager breasts?

The question of why Amis has created this disturbing double-take can only be addressed in the context of the maleness of the narrator and the implied reader. The murder narrative carries no explicit sexual overtones. These are conditional upon the gender and inclinations of the reader. The fourth stanza offers this reader a means of making them explicit. The images of violent control and sexual contact become intertwined.

'A Bookshop Idyll' is probably the most frequently quoted of Amis's 1950s poems, mainly because it seems to substantiate his popular image as an educated, tolerant misogynist. In fact he uses the poem to unsettle this persona. The narrator is in a bookshop and comes upon an anthology of contemporary poems whose titles seem to confirm his suspicion that women poets write candidly, transparently about their feelings, particularly their sexual feelings, while men can take it or leave it. These are the closing stanzas:

> We men have got love well weighed up; our stuff
>   Can get by without it
> Women don't seem to think that's good enough
>   They write about it,
>
> And the awful way their poems lay them open
>   Just doesn't strike them.
> Women are so much nicer than men:
>   No wonder we like them.

Deciding this, we can forget those times
    We sat up half the night
Chockfull of love, crammed with bright thoughts, names, rhymes,
    And couldn't write.

There is an ironic counterpoint between what Amis seems to say in this poem and the way he says it. His control of the verse form underpins the brash confidence of his thesis. The parallelism of the tight quatrains, particularly the sharp symmetry of the alternate short lines and the placing of semantic keynotes in rhyme positions – 'without it/about it', 'our stuff/good enough', 'strike them/like them' – recall the pseudo-logic of the Augustan couplet. The emotional vacuity and the questionable taste of the argument is sidelined by the persuasive force of the verse. The irony emerges in the final stanza and rolls back through what we have read. Amis comes close to admitting that on certain nights he 'couldn't write' because he couldn't bring himself to reconcile the intensity of his feelings with the confident and, as he concedes, male style which turns such feelings into a contrived effect – a style and an effect that are conspicuously evident in this poem.

'A Bookshop Idyll' would on the surface appear to conform to the manifesto of the Movement propounded by Robert Conquest in the Introduction to *New Lines* (1956). Poetry, he states, should be 'empirical in its attitude to all that comes', should 'resist the agglomeration of unconscious commands' and maintain 'a rational structure and comprehensible language'. 'A Bookshop Idyll' does all of this, but at the same time it uses its self-evident, confident familiarity to show us something else going on in the mind of the poet, something that exists on the edge of the empirical, the rational and the comprehensible.

'Nocturne' seems to be a 'Movement' poem par excellence, but again its stark realism incorporates delicate complexities of response.

> Under the winter street-lamps, near the bus stop,
> Two people with nowhere to go fondle each other,
> Writhe slowly in the entrance to a shop.
> In the intervals of watching them, a sailor
> Yaws about with an empty beer-flagon,
> Looking for something good to smash it on.

Mere animals: on this the Watch Committee
And myself seem likely to agree;
But all this fumbling about, this wasteful
Voiding of sweat and breath – is that *animal*?

Nothing so sure and economical.

These keep the image of another creature
In crippled versions, cocky, drab and stewed;
What beast holds off its paw to gesture,
Or gropes towards being understood?

The quality of this poem exists in its ability to interweave different levels of observation, feeling and reflection. In the first paragraph the scene is described with apparent indifference. The second provides a sardonic, then a more considered reflection upon the predictable verdict of the guardians of local decency. Finally the relationship between the observer and the characters observed becomes more ambiguous. The narrator's subtle differentiation of humans from animals as those who 'keep the image of another creature' applies both to the people under the street lamps and to himself. The writhing couple 'with nowhere else to go' have perhaps found temporary remission from this potential loneliness. This communicates itself to the drunken sailor who, motivated by witnessing what he does not have – 'In the intervals of watching them' – displaces his own despair into mindless aggression. Their behaviour might be less than decent but it is motivated by the human desire to 'keep the image of another', and we become gradually aware that the narrator himself is a participant·in this ritual of recognition and distance. The sense of isolation that motivates both the couple and the sailor is felt also by Amis and is displaced by him in a way that is appropriate to his role, as poet, but which nonetheless carries forward the sailor's search for 'something good to smash it on'. This turns out to be the closing passage of Yeats's 'A Second Coming' ('And what rough beast, its hour come round at last,/Slouches towards Bethlehem to be born?') which is echoed in the last two lines of 'Nocturne'. It is implied that Yeats, with his prediction of spiritual and moral decay, has much in common with the Watch Committee. Both regard anything that falls outside their utopian vision of

100

humanity as subhuman. Amis, without patronizing the couple and the sailor with symbol or analysis, at least recognizes their instincts and motivations as something that he shares.

In *A Case of Samples* Amis's verse is characterized by an effect similar to what happens when one photographic negative is laid upon another from the same reel, and when we see the same thing, simultaneously, in different ways. Both negatives will involve the same scene, but time will have passed between the two shots, the light and the perspective will have changed and the expressions on the faces of the people captured will have altered slightly. Amis achieves this effect in language by focusing the poem on a particular person, event or image while subtly shifting the perspective and obliging the reader to consider different attitudes and interpretations: parallax. The poems need to be read three or four times. During each subsequent encounter new levels of emotion and thought fold themselves into our first impression, and our understanding of what lies behind the writing of the poem deepens.

In *A Look Round the Estate* a polarity begins to emerge. Many of the poems employ the parallax effect, and just as many begin to move away from it, and settle for levels of irony, commentary and sardonic observation that are largely indifferent, and resonant of Betjeman.

By far the best of the latter is 'The Evans Country', a collection of poems involving the experiences of Dai Evans, a South Wales Everyman: young, old, father, son, JP and dissolute lecher. The poems take us back to the world of *That Uncertain Feeling* (1955). They involve idioms, habits and settings that are explicitly Welsh, but they neither patronize nor celebrate.

For examples of the parallax verse read 'Toys', 'Souvenirs', 'A Point of Logic' and 'Oligadora'. 'Toys' offers an image of shelves in a department store. On one side of the aisle are children's games and clothes. But,

> Across the aisle are tiers
> Of stuff we use on others
> As soon as we can: men's
> Two-tone cardigans;
> Earrings; rings; pens.

The contrast between two types of gift carries a resonance of

101

two types of feeling, two levels of endurance and commitment. The children's gifts of the first part are apparently as transient as their adult counterparts: the woollen ball and cuddly animal are 'expendable', the flame-proof nightdress 'pretty', the painting book will 'keep someone out of trouble'. Although it is never explicitly stated, the contrast between the two involves a deeper emotional level. The words 'expendable' and 'pretty' refer to the children's gifts, and as objects these will return year after year to the same shelves. What will not return are the children whom the speaker seems to be recalling. The adult gifts record a routine ritual, while the children's record a sense of loss. Their spatial division by the aisle is symbolic in the sense that it is occupied by the speaker, who is literally and figuratively caught between the past and immediate experience, both involving conflicts between feeling and gesture, memory and the present, lost experience and mundane actuality. These emotive currents are never engaged with explicitly. Instead, individual words – particularly 'expendable' and 'pretty' – react with the cool, objective mood of documentation and listing in the same way that an Imagist poem generates a possibility of profound emotion from discontinuous juxtapositions. The poem is at once suggestive and elliptical, inviting an enquiry into the sensitive, painful condition of the speaker, and at the same time resisting it.

'A Point of Logic' invites comparison with 'Alternatives'. Two verse paragraphs describe the same act. The first has a man and a woman climbing stairs to the bedroom, stairs of 'marble/Or decently scrubbed boards'. Our situation, Amis tells us, 'Teaches us who we are/And what we are' just as much as 'what we do'. In the second paragraph he advises us to 'put out the light'.

> Lurch to the bare attic
> Over buckets of waste
> And labouring bodies;
> Leave the door wide open
> And fall on each other;

The impression is of a contrast between the established, finished environment of the first part and the sense in the second of a house, and by implication a relationship, being built, full of energy and honest desire. But at the end this neat polarity is withdrawn.

> Stay only a minute
> Depart separately,
> And use no names.

The technique is the same as in 'Alternatives': the closing section rolls back and alters our first impression. The phrases 'buckets of waste' and 'labouring bodies' become endlessly ambiguous: builder's waste and toiling builders, or human waste and strenuous, public, sex? When we first encounter the 'bare attic' and the wish to 'leave the door wide open', they contribute to the notion of a couple celebrating their future, perhaps in their new home. What will the attic become? A nursery, perhaps. And who cares if the builders can hear us through the open door – we're in love. The last lines change all of this. It could be a half-built house, but one chosen for the sake of convenience by a couple who do not know each other and never will. Or it could be a catalogue of degenerate fantasies; real only in the sense that they provide an appropriate mental counterpart to the moment of anonymous sex, wherever it occurs. The uncertainty is compounded when we return to 'Therefore, put out the light' at the beginning of the second paragraph. Perhaps the entire narrative of uncommitted sex is a fantasy, something to imagine during the domesticated version, to make it more exciting. In 'Alternatives' the different narratives combine to create an uneasy effect; in 'A Point of Logic' our unease begins when we attempt to distinguish between the real, the imagined, the figurative and the fantastic.

'Nothing to Fear' is an account of the thoughts that run through the mind of a man in a flat 'Lent by a friend, whose note says *Lucky sod*'. He is waiting for a woman: 'the cover story pat/ And quite uncheckable; her husband off/Somewhere with the kids till six o'clock'. He reflects with covetous glee on her impressive face, legs, hips and breasts, and at the end of the first paragraph he dismisses feelings of guilt, compunction and 'all that cock;/It'll wear off, as usual'. But it does not, and in the second paragraph the pace of the language quickens as he asks himself why he feels so uneasy: 'this slight trembling,/Dry mouth, quick pulse rate, sweaty hands/As though she were the first?' The sense of unease that he had earlier dismissed becomes tangibly present in the closing lines:

                    sitting here, a bag of glands
              Tuned up to concert pitch, I seem to sense
              A different style of caller at my back,
              As cold as ice, but just as set on me.

The poem is autobiographical. Amis in the fifties and early sixties made use of his friend Robert Conquest's London flat for numerous adulterous liaisons. His habits were the major factor in the temporary breakdown of his marriage with Hilly, which occurred around the time that this poem was written. It is a transparent poem, in that it does not need to be explored for a particular meaning, but at the same time it captures a sensation that can only be explained in terms of the events that cause it. Conventional guilt, which he can cope with, is transformed into a fear of something that can only be himself, a figure who lives two lives and is rightly terrified at the thought of their intersection. The 'different style of caller' disturbs the self-contained pleasure of the illicit liaison which the rest of the poem tries so desperately to celebrate.

Many of the parallax poems of the 1950s and early 1960s are concerned with sexuality, often using images of unrestrained hedonism as counterpoints to the conventions of ordinary, settled existence – virtually a mirror image of Amis's life with Hilly. 'Nothing to Fear' and more obliquely 'A Point of Logic' signal the end of the double-life upon which the parallax poems draw. The unspoken emotional crisis addressed in the closing lines of the former is more explicitly realized in the latter: both involve an anxious shuffling of emotion and desire. After this the double perspective disappeared almost entirely from Amis's poetry and the double-life from his relationships. Hilly left him in 1963. In the same year he moved in with Elizabeth Jane Howard, and they married in 1965. He was mostly faithful to Jane and their relationship broke down in the late 1970s not because of Amis's desire for other women but because of his lack of desire for any woman. In 1979 he wrote to Larkin of his 'total loss of sex drive; I haven't had a fuck for more than a year and a wank for over a month', and in 1980 of why Jane had left him: 'partly to punish me for stopping wanting to fuck her and partly because she realised I didn't like her very much'.[1]

All of this provided ample background material for *Jake's Thing* (1979), but the parallels between Amis's life and his poetry,

104

while less explicit, are far more intriguing.

The ending of his double-life and his eventual loss of interest in sex is mirrored in his poetry by the emergence of a persona who is single-mindedly Augustan in his perspectives upon the world. In 'Senex', written in the late 1970s, Amis compares his own loss of sex drive with the same thing experienced by Sophocles. For Sophocles this was 'no disaster/He said he felt like one released/From service with a cruel master'. But for Amis: 'I envy him – I miss the lash/At which I used to snort and snivel'. The poem is candid, but it involves the kind of candour that Pope perfected in his 'Epistle to Dr Arbuthnot'. Pope is disarmingly honest in his autobiographical musings, but by wrapping his disclosures in his self-focused wit he also disarms the more complex emotions that might have attended them.

> The Muse but served to ease some friend, not wife,
> To help me through this long disease, my life.

These lines record Pope's experience of poetry and lonely bachelorhood, and Amis tells of his own desexualized state. Both are polished, sardonic, self-mocking, and at the same time protective of the kind of feelings that cannot easily be reduced to the cool ironies of the public poem.

Amis, like Pope, knew that this mode of writing was best employed as a means of observing the world through the kind of satiric, journalistic lens where dark humour is balanced against distressing actuality.

'The Huge Artifice: an interim assessment' is, recalling Swift's 'Verses on the Death of Dr Swift', an ironic, self-referential consideration of Amis's fiction of the fifties and early sixties. It gathers in the dismissive pomposity of his most hostile reviewers: 'the main purpose – *what it's all about*/In the thematic sense – remains in doubt'. The plot is 'thin, repetitive', involving that 'excessive use of coincidence/Which betrays authorial inexperience'. There is a figure in an early episode 'who/Was clearly introduced in order to/Act as some kind of author surrogate,/Then hastily killed off', which could of course be Jim Dixon, who, as Amis knows, has never really died. There are 'gaps in sensitivity', a 'habit of indifference' which makes 'the gentle come to grief' (Jenny Bunn?). All of which contribute to 'An inhumanity beyond despair'.

105

The closing verse paragraph almost qualifies these condemnations by conceding that some readers have found characters who are 'not quite submerged/In all this rubbish'. But does this 'exculpate the mind/that was their author'?

> Not at all. We find
> Many of these in the history of art
> (So this reviewer feels), who stand apart,
> Who by no purpose of their own begin
> To struggle free from a base origin.

What better praise could there be but for a reviewer to declare that the only decent, human elements of an author's work are too good, too real, to have come from his imagination?

The poem, like Swift's, is probably Amis's most forthright declaration of his own literary qualities. Amis, via the hostile reviewer, condemns himself for strenuously avoiding moral, philosophical or thematic cohesion. But his tongue is calculatedly in cheek. There is, beneath the withering condemnation, Amis's fundamental principle of writing: only by refusing to make the represented world conform to ideals and analytical theses can the author disclose its, albeit infrequent, qualities.

In 'New Approach Needed' Amis addresses Jesus Christ on our saviour's failure to properly experience the human condition. True he had 'heard about' hunger, disease, madness, war, love, marriage and having children, but he did not know what they felt like. Amis advises him to next time 'come off' the cross,

> And get some service in,
> Jack, long before you start
> Laying down the old law;
> If you still want to then.
> Tell your dad that from me.

The mood, the iconoclastic wit, is consistent with Amis's treatment of Christianity in his novels, and, as in most of the novels, Amis the performer just displaces Amis the private person.

'Shitty' begins by asking an unidentified addressee to 'Look thy last' on the shittiness of Britain in the sixties and seventies: pop groups, cultish admiration for Mao and Che Guevara, women wearing what appear to be curtains and blankets. It ends:

106

> High rise blocks and action paintings
> Sculptures made from wire and lead
> Each of these a sight more lovely
> Than the screens around your bed.

The poem is like an extended version of an Augustan couplet. Amis offers us a typically nasty, confidently reactionary vision of what life has become, and then turns the mirror on his subject: life is full of pretentious banalities but leaving it is worse. It recalls passages from Dryden's Translations of Lucretius's *De Rerum Natura*,

> And therefore if a man bemoan his lot
> That after death his mouldering limbs shall rot,
> Or flames or jaws of beasts devour his mass,
> Know, he's an unsincere, unthinking ass...
> He boasts no sense can after death remain,
> Yet makes himself a part of life again...

(ll. 49–56)

Both poems work by contrasting the emotive polarities of the human condition. They unsettle and shock the reader: but the real complexities of their topics – on how we deal with death – are transformed into a cool demonstration of how the gifted poetry technician deals with death.

This method of juxtaposing emotional states reappears in extended form in 'Their Oxford'. Amis takes us through the Oxford of the 1970s with each part of the city recalling memories of his own student days. He does not romanticize the past, but he prefers it.

> In my day there were giants on the scene
> Men big enough to be worth laughing at:
> Coghill and Bowra, Lewis and Tolkien.
> Lost confidence and envy finished that.

At the end he half concedes that the middle-aged resent the present not because the past was different or better, but because it has gone. One gets the impression that Amis is more concerned with using the poem as a polished rerun of this unoriginal reflection rather than for telling us anything new about it.

Amis employs the modern Augustan mode most effectively in 'South'. Part I shows us a land of fantastic beauty.

New wonders, but familiar in the mind,
A world of greenwood without end
God's England.

Gradually he introduces the twentieth century: 'ranch-style, eat-o-mat, drive in, Headlight, tail-light, floodlight, neon'. All this would be tolerable, but for 'the voice/Of something vicious': Southern American racism.

You blind? Can't you see they're inferior –
Our women's what they're really after –
You got to use fear –
. . . .

In the libraries, books about justice,
Freedom, innocence, goodness.
No use.

This is unashamed, polemical, political verse. It uses literary devices, in that each clipped stanza tears away another layer of the original façade of bucolic bliss. It is a distilled example of the tradition of Dryden's 'Absalom and Achitophel'. Its form re-enacts its engagement with duplicity and hypocrisy, but its conclusions are unambiguous.

The shared characteristic of much of this later verse is its disclosure of a speaker whose opinions on the world are captured by his texts, but who at the same time takes a step back. They are written by Kingsley Amis the public poet, whereas the persona who inhabited the earlier, parallax poems brought into them the less secure presence of Kingsley Amis the man, someone for whom the poem was not so much a statement or an exercise, but more an exploration of things unresolved, undecided and only half understood. He would return, briefly.

Amis's *You Can't Do Both* (1994) is his most autobiographical novel, and at its centre is his sense of regret and loss at the collapse of his marriage to Hilly. Two of his later poems echo the novel in their uncluttered, yet uncertain, transparency. 'Wasted', written in the late 1970s, tells of a 'cold winter evening' when the fire would not draw. The family gather around the rain-soaked logs in the 'dismal' grate, and after they have gone to bed, the speaker, alone, watches as 'The wood began to flame/In clear rose and violet/Heating the small hearth'. In the last four lines he asks,

> Why should that memory cling
> Now the children are all grown up
> And the house – a different house –
> Is warm at any season?

The memory endures because it is not really a memory; it is about the way that he feels now. The fire catches, but only when they have all gone away, and he is on his own in a 'different house'.

Amis's last poem, number III of a sequence called 'To H', (published in *Memoirs*, 1991) is like nothing he had written before. There are no conceits, and it employs, quite beautifully, the kind of free verse line that cannot be reduced to a technical formula. It is about Hilly,

> Whose eye I could have met for ever then,
> Oh yes, and who was also beautiful.
> Well, that was much as women were meant to be,
> I thought, and set about looking further.
> How can we tell, with nothing to compare?

The last three words roll back through the open simplicity of the poem and split the perspective. Until the last line, the verb phrases are in the past tense. Hilly, he has told us, was incomparable. Yet the present tense 'can', brings us back to the speaker in the text, left now with nothing to compare.

Notes

CHAPTER 1. INTRODUCING KINGSLEY AMIS

1. Gilbert Phelps, 'The Novel Today', in *The Penguin Guide to English Literature*, vol. 7, *The Modern Age* (London: Penguin, 1973), 510–13.
2. Roger Fowler, *Linguistics and the Novel* (London: Routledge & Kegan Paul, 1977).
3. Tom Paulin, 'The Cruelty that is Natural' in *Ireland and the English Crisis* (Newcastle-upon-Tyne: Bloodaxe, 1984), 45.
4. Gabriel Josipovici, *The World and the Book* (London: Macmillan, 1971).
5. David Lodge, *The Modes of Modern Writing: Metaphor, Metonymy and the Typology of Modern Fiction* (London: Routledge & Kegan Paul, 1977), 52.

CHAPTER 2. METHOD AND DEVELOPMENT

1. David Lodge, 'The Modern, the Contemporary and the Importance of Being Amis', in *The Language of Fiction* (London: Routledge & Kegan Paul, 1966).
2. *G. K. Chesterton: Selected Stories* (London: Penguin, 1973), 15.
3. Michael Radcliffe, review in *The Times*, 11 October 1969.
4. Interview in *Contemporary Literature*, 16 January 1975.
5. 'Four Fluent Fellows: An Essay on Chesterton's Fiction', in *G. K. Chesterton, a Centenary Appraisal*, ed. J. Sullivan (London: Paul Elek, 1973), 28.
6. 'Fit to Kill', *New Statesman*, 22 September 1978, 384.
7. Reprinted in Kingsley Amis, *What Became of Jane Austen? and Other Questions* (London: Jonathan Cape, 1970).

CHAPTER 3. SEX

1. Review in the *Sunday Times*, 20 May 1984.

2.   *Listener*, 20 February 1975, 240–41.

CHAPTER 4. OPINIONS: POLITICS, NATION, GOD, CLASS AND RACE

1.   *What Became of Jane Austen?*, 86.
2.   *An Arts Policy?* (London: Centre for Policy Studies, 1979), 3.
3.   *What Became of Jane Austen?*, 51.
4.   *New Statesman*, 22 September 1978, 384.
5.   'Real and Made Up People', *Times Literary Supplement*, 27 July 1973, 847–8.
6.   Paulin, 44–6.

CHAPTER 5. POETRY

1.   Eric Jacobs, *Kingsley Amis: A Biography* (London: Hodder & Stoughton, 1995), 316, 324.

Select Bibliography

WORKS BY KINGSLEY AMIS

Novels
Lucky Jim (London: Victor Gollancz, 1954).
That Uncertain Feeling (London: Victor Gollancz, 1955).
I Like It Here (London: Victor Gollancz, 1958).
Take a Girl Like You (London: Victor Gollancz, 1960).
One Fat Englishman (London: Victor Gollancz, 1963).
The Egyptologists, with Robert Conquest (London: Jonathan Cape, 1965).
The Anti-Death League (London: Victor Gollancz, 1966).
Colonel Sun, as Robert Markham (London: Jonathan Cape, 1968).
I Want It Now (London: Jonathan Cape, 1968).
The Green Man (London: Jonathan Cape, 1969).
Girl, 20 (London: Jonathan Cape, 1971).
The Riverside Villas Murder (London: Jonathan Cape, 1973).
Ending Up (London: Jonathan Cape, 1974).
The Alteration (London: Jonathan Cape, 1976).
Jake's Thing (London: Hutchinson, 1978).
Russian Hide-and-Seek (London: Hutchinson, 1980).
Stanley and the Women (London: Hutchinson, 1984).
The Old Devils (London: Hutchinson, 1986).
The Crime of the Century (London: J. M. Dent, 1987).
Difficulties with Girls (London: Hutchinson, 1988).
The Folks That Live on the Hill (London: Hutchinson, 1990).
The Russian Girl (London: Hutchinson, 1992).
You Can't Do Both (London: Hutchinson, 1994).
The Biographer's Moustache (London: HarperCollins, 1995).

Poetry
Bright November (London: Fortune Press, 1947).
A Frame of Mind (Reading: School of Art, University of Reading, 1953).

Kingsley Amis: No. 22, The Fantasy Poets (Oxford: Fantasy Press, 1954).
A Case of Samples: Poems 1946–1956 (London: Victor Gollancz, 1956).
The Evans Country (Oxford: Fantasy Press, 1962).
A Look Round the Estate: Poems 1957–1967 (London: Jonathan Cape, 1967).
Collected Poems 1944–1979 (London: Hutchinson, 1979; Viking Press, 1980).

Short stories
My Enemy's Enemy (London: Victor Gollancz, 1962).
Dear Illusion (London: Covent Garden Press, 1972).
The Darkwater Hall Mystery (Edinburgh, Tragara Press, 1978).
Collected Short Stories (London: Hutchinson, 1980; 1987, including 'Investing in Futures' and 'Affairs of Death').

Criticism
New Maps of Hell: A Survey of Science Fiction (New York: Harcourt Brace, 1960; London: Victor Gollancz, 1961).
What Became of Jane Austen? and Other Questions (London: Jonathan Cape, 1970).
'Four Fluent Fellows: An Essay on Chesterton's Fiction', in *G. K. Chesterton, a Centenary Appraisal*, ed. J. Sullivan (London: Paul Elek, 1973).

Works edited or with contributions by Amis
Oxford Poetry 1949, with James Michie (Oxford: Basil Blackwell, 1949).
G. K. Chesterton: Selected Stories (London and Boston: Faber & Faber, 1972).
Tennyson, Poet to Poet series (London: Penguin, 1973).
Introduction to G. K. Chesterton, *The Man Who Was Thursday* (London: Penguin, 1986).

Miscellaneous writings
Socialism and the Intellectuals (London: Fabian Society, 1957).
Lucky Jim's Politics (London: Conservative Political Centre, 1968).
An Arts Policy? (London: Centre for Policy Studies, 1979).
The Amis Collection (London: Hutchinson, 1990).
Memoirs (London: Hutchinson, 1991)
The Kings English: A Guide to Modern Usage (London: HarperCollins, 1997).

BOOKS AND ESSAYS ON AMIS

There are five book-length critical studies of Amis. All are straightforward, generally admiring, surveys of his writing:

Bradford, Richard, *Kingsley Amis* (London: Edward Arnold, 1989).

Gardner, Philip, *Kingsley Amis* (Boston: Twayne, 1981).

McDermott, John, *Kingsley Amis: An English Moralist* (London: Macmillan, 1989).

Moseley, Merritt, *Understanding Kingsley Amis* (South Carolina University Press, 1993).

Salwak, Dale, *Kingsley Amis: Modern Novelist* (London: Harvester, 1992).

Two books give more emphasis to Amis the man:

Fussell, Paul, *The Anti-Egotist: Kingsley Amis, Man of Letters* (Oxford: Oxford University Press, 1994). This is an engaging study of the man and his work by someone who knew him well for thirty years.

Jacobs, Eric, *Kingsley Amis: A Biography* (London: Hodder & Stoughton, 1995). An honest, very readable account of his life, approved by Amis himself.

Several books and essays offer comparative, contextual accounts of British writing in the 1950s and early 1960s, and Amis's place within these trends.

Allsop, Kenneth, *The Angry Decade* (London: Peter Owen, 1958). The title speaks for itself.

Caplan, Ralph, 'Kingsley Amis', *Contemporary British Novelists*, ed. C. Shapiro (Southern Illinois University Press, 1965), ch. 1. Considers the first five novels as examples of 'serious' comedy.

Gindin, James, *Post-War British Fiction* (Cambridge: Cambridge University Press, 1962). Another book which deals with the comic realism of Amis's writings of the 1950s.

Morrison, Blake, *The Movement* (Oxford: Oxford University Press, 1980). Offers a detailed account of British poetry and fiction of the 1950s.

Rabinowitz, Rubin, *The Reaction Against Experiment in the English Novel: 1950–1960* (New York: Columbia University Press, 1967). Particularly good on critical reactions to Amis's early fiction.

The following are more recent surveys of post-war fiction, which include discussions of Amis's work since the 1950s. D. J. Taylor's book is the most recent and original account of post-war fiction, and Amis's place in it.

Bergonzi, Bernard, *The Situation of the Novel* (London: Macmillan, 1970).

Green, Martin, *The English Novel in the Twentieth Century* (London: Routledge & Kegan Paul, 1984).

McEwan, Neil, *The Survival of the Novel: British Fiction in the Later 20th Century* (London, Macmillan, 1981).

Stevenson, Randall, *The British Novel Since the Thirties* (London: Batsford,

1986).

Swinden, Patrick, *The English Novel of History and Society, 1940–1980* (London: Macmillan, 1984).

Taylor, D. J., *After the War: the Novel and English Society Since 1945* (London: Chatto and Windus, 1993).

OTHER WORKS CITED IN THE TEXT

Fowler, Roger, *Linguistics and the Novel* (London: Routledge & Kegan Paul, 1977).

Josipovici, Gabriel, *The World and the Book* (London: Macmillan, 1971).

Lodge, David, 'The Modern, the Contemporary and the Importance of Being Amis', in *The Language of Fiction* (London: Routledge & Kegan Paul, 1966).

Lodge, David, *The Modes of Modern Writing: Metaphor, Metonymy and the Typology of Modern Fiction* (London: Routledge & Kegan Paul, 1977).

Paulin, Tom, 'The Cruelty that is Natural', an article on *Jake's Thing*, reprinted in *Ireland and the English Crisis* (Newcastle-upon-Tyne: Bloodaxe, 1984).

Phelps, Gilbert, 'The Novel Today', in *The Penguin Guide to English Literature*, vol. 7, *The Modern Age* (London: Penguin, 1973).

Index

America, 18–19, 31, 32, 41–2, 57,
85, 107–8
Amis, Kingsley,
NOVELS
Alteration, The, 5, 31–3, 63, 82
Anti-Death League, The, 5, 19–
24, 61–2, 80, 82, 92
Biographer's Moustache, The,
48–9, 77–9
Difficulties with Girls, 42, 61,
66, 69–71
Ending Up, 36–7, 47, 61
Folks That Live on the Hill, The,
46–7
Girl, 20, 37, 85–7
Green Man, The, 5, 8, 24–31, 51,
62, 80–1, 82
I Like It Here, 17–18, 81–2
I Want It Now, 37, 85
Jake's Thing, 6, 37–9, 40–1, 45,
60, 63–5, 87-90, 91, 104
Lucky Jim, 1, 3, 4, 5, 7, 10–16,
19, 42, 49, 60, 72–3, 81, 105
Old Devils, The, 7, 41–2, 61,
83–4
One Fat Englishman, 18–19, 61,
76
Riverside Villas Murder, The, 61
Russian Girl, The, 42–5
Russian Hide and Seek, 33–6
Stanley and the Women, 6, 9,
39–41, 45, 57–60, 65–6

Take a Girl Like You, 5, 18, 23,
42, 61, 66–9, 77–8, 105
That Uncertain Feeling, 16–17,
39, 60–1, 73–6, 82, 101
You Can't Do Both, 47–8, 108

SHORT STORIES
'I Spy Strangers', 50
'Mason's Life', 55–6
'Moral Fibre', 50
'The Darkwater Hall Mystery',
53
'The House on the Headland',
55
'To See the Sun', 53
'Who or What Was It?', 51–3

POEMS
'A Bookshop Idyll', 98–9
'A Point of Logic', 101, 102–3
'A Song of Experience', 96–7
'Against Romanticism', 95
'Alternatives', 97–8
'Bed and Breakfast', 94–5
'Belgian Winter', 94
'Beowulf', 94
'Letter to Elisabeth', 92–4
'New Approach Needed', 106
'Nocturne', 99–101
'Nothing to Fear', 103–4
'Oligadora', 101
'Radar', 94

'Senex', 105
'Shitty', 106–7
'South', 107–8
'Souvenirs', 101
'The Evans Country', 101
'The Huge Artifice: an
    interim assessment', 105–6
'Their Oxford', 107
'To H', 109
'Toys', 101–2
'Wasted', 108–9

MISCELLANEOUS
Amis Collection, The, 8
An Arts Policy?, 72, 78–9
G. K. Chesterton, Selected Stories
    (ed.), 24
'Four Fluent Fellows', 33
'Godforsaken', 1
'Kipling Good', 42–3
Legacy, The, 3
Memoirs, 1, 8, 46, 109
Socialism and the Intellectuals,
    72, 76
Tennyson, 2
What Became of Jane Austen?, 8
'Where Tawe Flows', 82–3
'Why Lucky Jim Turned
    Right', 9, 72

'Angry Young Men, The', 4, 73
Auden, W. H., 92–3, 94
Austen, Jane, 90

Bailey, John, 36
Bardwell, Hilary Ann (Hilly), 2,
    45, 48, 104, 107–8
Bardwell, Leonard, 45
Barstow, Stan, 77
Beckett, Samuel, 38, 81
Betjeman, John, 101
Bevan, Nye, 17
Blake, William, 32, 96

Boyd, Alastair, Lord Kilmarnock,
    46
Braine, John, 4, 73, 77
Browning, Robert, 2
Buck, Pearl S., 70

Carey, John, 57–8
Caton, L. S. (and) Reginald
    Ashley, 92
Chekhov, Anton, 34
Chesterton, G. K., 24, 33
Conan Doyle, Arthur, 53
Conquest, Robert, 3, 51, 99, 104

Davie, Donald, 3
Dickens, Charles, 32, 90
Dostoyevsky, Fyodor, 34, 43
Dryden, John, 107–8
du Maurier, Daphne, 70

Eliot, T. S., 92–3, 96
Enright, D. J., 3

Fielding, Henry, 13–14, 70–1
Forster, E. M., 90
Fowler, Roger, 5–6
Freud, Sigmund, 88
Fuller, Roy, 92

Harrison, Tony, 97
Hoggart, Richard, 75
Hockney, David, 32
Hopkins, Gerard Manley, 2
Howard, Elizabeth Jane, 51–2, 66,
    104
Huxley, Aldous, 22, 31

Jacobs, Eric, 48, 49, 66
James, Henry, 18
Jenkins, Roy, 62
Johnson, B. S., 30
Jones, Monica, 45
Josipovici, Gabriel, 6–7
Joyce, James, 24, 81

Laing, R. D., 58
Larkin, Philip, 1, 3, 45, 83, 92, 95, 104
Lawrence, D.H., 18, 79, 81
Leavis, F. R., 5
Lewis, Alun, 92
Lewis, C. S., 92
Llewellyn, Richard, 75
Lodge, David, 8, 11, 90

Maugham, W. Somerset, 11, 81
Meredith, George, 2
Millett, Kate, 57, 71
Milton, John, 28–30
Morris, William, 2
'Movement' The, 3, 73, 95, 99
Murdoch, Iris, 27, 81

O'Casey, Sean, 88, 89
Orwell, George, 11, 31, 90
Osborne, John, 4, 73

Paulin, Tom, 6, 91
Phelps, Gilbert, 5
Pinter, Harold, 38
Pope, Alexander, 5, 105
Private Eye, 10

Rossetti, Dante Gabriel, 2

Sartre, Jean-Paul, 32

Shakespeare, William, 32, 35–6, 37, 97
Sillitoe, Alan, 73, 77
Sinclair, Andrew, 30–1
Spark, Muriel, 36
Storey, David, 73
Swift, Jonathan, 5, 31, 105–6

Taylor, Elizabeth, 70
Tennyson, Alfred, Lord, 2
Thackeray, William Makepeace, 90
Thatcher, Margaret, 72, 73, 76
Thomas, Dylan, 16, 18, 41, 74, 83, 92, 94
Tolstoy, L. N., 34
Trevor, William, 36

Wales, 16–17, 41–2, 73–5, 82–4, 101
Wain, John, 4
Waugh, Evelyn, 10–11, 18, 22, 27, 33, 79–80, 90
Welles Orson, 51
Wilson, Colin, 73
Wodehouse, P. G., 11
Woolf, Virginia, 7, 24
Wordsworth, William, 96

Yeats, W. B., 100
Yevtushenko, Yevgeny, 43.